SCOTTISH URBAN LEGENDS
50 MYTHS AND TRUE STORIES

AARON MULLINS

The information provided in this book is designed to entertain the reader on the subjects discussed. Although the author has made every effort to ensure that the information in this book was correct at time of press, the author does not assume and hereby disclaims any liability to any party for any loss, damage, or disruption caused by errors or omissions. Much of the information contained within these stories is available in a wide variety of forms within the public domain. Other tales were whispered to the author by friends and mysterious acquaintances. It has been gathered together into a unique creative writing piece, told in the author's own words, for the sole purpose of entertainment.

ISBN: 9798550033333

PRAISE FOR AARON MULLINS

"**One of Scotland's best writers**"
Amazon Review

"**A master of the psychological thriller**"
Amazon Review

"Ayrshire author shines"
Daily Record

"Aaron has emerged as **one of Scotland's
most popular up-and-coming authors**"
Inverness Courier

"Stories that will pull you in, fast paced with twists and turns"
Amazon Review

"**Aaron Mullins is a compelling story-teller**"
Amazon Review

"I really enjoyed reading this book, very thought provoking"
Amazon Review

"**Brilliant stories**, really is something for everyone in there"
Smashwords Review

"Novel races up the Amazon book charts"
Ayrshire Post

"**I could not put this down**, the author just pulled you in from
the very first page. Each story makes you stop and think about
life and friendships"
Amazon Review

"Aaron hits top 100 list with Highland mystery tales"
John O'Groat Journal

"Tales of mythical beasties tops charts"
Troon Times

"The book was **a top 10 bestseller**… sitting alongside books by
Neil Gaiman and Stephen King"
The Orkney News

"These short stories just pull you in from the very first page.
Brilliant stories with something for everyone to enjoy"
Amazon Review

"It has already featured in the Amazon top 100 bestsellers…
alongside books by Stephen King and Dean Koontz"
Press and Journal

"If you love **suspense with good humour** then look no further"
Amazon Review

"**Very well written**, as you would expect from an Aaron Mullins
book, and gives you just enough of a tingle down your spine!!"
Amazon Review

"engrossing and **entertaining collection** of short stories
…would make a five-star-rating popular TV drama series
…**universal storytelling at its best**"
– Review by Carol McKay (author and reader for The Highland Book
Prize) of *Mysteries and Misadventures: Tales from the Highlands*

"His love for the Highlands and its people shines through, both
in his stories and reflections on his personal journey"
Caithness Courier

"They arrive like sprites. Whispering in his ear, buzzing around
in his mind, walking around his consciousness... The shadows at
the edge, the inspiration for his next writing project"
Ayrshire Magazine (Interview with Aaron Mullins)

DEDICATION

This book is dedicated to those who keep the art of storytelling alive. The people who huddle around the campfire on a chilly winter's evening to swap tales of wonder. The modern Midnight Society.

"Stories have to be told or they die, and when they die, we can't remember who we are or why we're here."

- Sue Monk Kidd

Also by Aaron Mullins

FICTION
Mysteries and Misadventures: Tales from the Highlands
Scottish Urban Legends: 50 Myths and True Stories
Scottish Legends: 55 Mythical Monsters
Scottish Killers: 25 True Crime Stories
Mullins Collection of Best New Fiction
Mullins Collection of Best New Horror

WRITING GUIDES
How to Write Fiction: A Creative Writing Guide for Authors

BUSINESS GUIDES
How to Write a Business Plan
The Ultimate Business Plan Template

PSYCHOLOGY
The Effect of Mate Value on Self-esteem
Social Responsibility and Community Resilience
Risk Perception in Extreme Event Decision Making
Ethnic Differences in Perceptions of Social Responsibility
and many more…

www.aaronmullins.com

CONTENTS

PREFACE

Scotland has always been a land filled with magic, myths and mystery. Its rich history has created many folk tales and legends that have been passed down through the generations. Amongst these myths lurk true stories and things I have witnessed with my own eyes, all captured within this anthology.

I was inspired to write this collection by a story from my previous book *Mysteries and Misadventures: Tales from the Highlands.* For the story *Call of the Nuckelavee,* I delved deep into researching mythical Orcadian creatures, which led me down the rabbit hole of reading about Scottish urban legends.

I then discussed the true 'Story Behind the Stories' at the end of the book, which hinted at childhood urban legends from my home town. *The House on Lovers' Lane* story was also inspired by the legend of *Tam o' Shanter* by Robert Burns. So it seemed I was destined to follow the thread of intrigue to the next logical step.

One evening I messaged my friends asking them about their own favourite myths and tales. I was reminded about the ghostly urban legends surrounding my primary school, which have made their way into this book. Everybody I asked had their own haunting tale to tell.

All of these stories were swirling around inside my head and I knew that I wanted to give them my own spin, do some research and collect the most interesting ones together into an anthology. So here we are.

Thanks go, as always, to my editorial and research support team of Matthew, Stuart and Christopher. I tell them my idea and they help me shape it into a book, suggesting additions and digging out links to long-forgotten resources. Thank you also to those friends who recommended tales to research as we terrified each other with reminders of childhood beliefs and superstitions. And endless gratitude to Lil for her incredible eye for detail and insightful support.

The true power of these Scottish tales lies in their ability to not only entertain us in the present but to forge a link to our past. From tales of great battles to pagan rituals that are still performed today, new generations can enjoy the stories and feel connected to the land and its people.

Some of the stories have morals to teach us, lessons learnt by our ancestors and told around campfires. Ancient warriors live on, still marching to the echoes of war drums beating with every re-telling of their accomplishments.

I have not included many tales about Scotland's legendary creatures. As you can imagine, a country that has a unicorn as its national animal has a whole host of legends and stories about mythical creatures. I have given these tales the focus they deserve in a book solely dedicated to them. You can find *Scottish Legends: 55 Mythical Monsters* alongside my other books.

I have included well-known urban legends along with local myths and stories that are touted as being true. Let's gather around the fire, listen to the tales and decide for ourselves.

Aaron Mullins

www.aaronmullins.com

CHAPTER 1

HAUNTED HOMES

G hosts are often believed to attach themselves to places that were important to them in life, or were the scene of their death. They are said to haunt many homes, castles and other buildings across Scotland.

The Devil himself may frequent your home, or perhaps that shadow moving in the hallway may have a more earthly and deadly explanation.

This chapter explores some of the urban legends that have sprung up around these places, because there is more than just the paranormal lurking within their walls.

THE HOUSE OF THE BINNS

During the 17th century, General Tam Dalyell (pronounced *dee el*) was the head of the Dalyell family and founder of the Royal Scots Greys, a cavalry regiment of the British Army. Legend has it that he was also an opponent of the Devil in a nightly game of cards.

As Commander-in-Chief of the King's forces in Scotland, he was a well-known and respected figure. He had escaped after being imprisoned in the Tower of London following the Battle of Worcester. Fleeing to Russia, he served Tsar Alexis I and is thought to have been responsible for introducing the thumbscrew torture device to Britain.

His service in the Russian military earned him the nickname *The Muscovite De'il*. Following the Pentland Rising at Rullion Green, 1,200 captured Covenanters were imprisoned and tortured in Greyfriars Kirkyard. This earned Tam another nickname, *Bluidy Tam*. Little surprise then that the Devil would choose such an opponent with whom to play a hand of cards after dark.

After returning to Scotland, it was Tam himself that claimed the Devil would visit him each night at his ancestral family home, the House of the Binns. The land the ancient house sits upon, situated in West Lothian, may have once held a Pictish fort, with written records from 1335 referring to the *Bynnis*.

As hikers of the Scottish hillsides may be aware, the house derives its name from the two hills its estate encompasses, as the Gaelic *ben, beinn or bheinn* (for mountain or peak –

think Ben Nevis, Ben Lomond etc...) has become *House of the Bens*, later becoming *Binns*, literally meaning *House of the Hills*. This is just one of a handful of Gaelic words which are useful to know when perusing a UK Ordnance Survey map of Scotland to plan your adventure, as they give clues to the terrain you'll likely encounter.

However, the maps won't indicate what type of foul and beastly creatures you may meet on your journey. And Bluidy Tam had seemingly befriended the Prince of Darkness himself.

The Devil was an excellent card player and would win their nightly games, much to Tam's annoyance. One night Tam was dealt the perfect hand and managed to beat the Devil, but did so by employing devious means, with a mirror placed behind the table to reveal his fiendish opponent's cards.

After finally losing and discovering that Tam had cheated, the Devil was enraged and launched the heavy marble table at Tam. The table missed Tam, broke through a window and ended up sinking into the Sergeant's Pond outside Tam's stately home.

When Tam told others of his nightly visits he was ridiculed. The table was simply listed as being missing and eventually forgotten about

The pond was too deep to explore at that time. Nobody would accept he played cards with the Devil and Tam died without anybody ever believing him.

However, over two hundred years later there was a summer drought and the Sergeant's Pond outside the House of the Binns dried up.

And there, nestled into the mud at the bottom of the pond, was a heavy marble table.

It's said that this story came to light when the mother of the twentieth century Tam Dalyell asked a local joiner if he would repair the legs on a marble table owned by the family. When the tradesman arrived at the estate, he discovered that in order to repair the legs, he must first retrieve the table from the bottom of the pond.

Intriguingly, the paranormal tales of the House of the Binns did not end with Tam's death.

It's said that at night a ghostly rider can be seen and heard galloping on a white stallion along the road that leads to the house. And if you listen closely (and are brave enough to leave your bed) you might just see Tam's cavalry boots marching around the house by themselves.

You can investigate these paranormal occurrences for yourself by visiting the House of the Binns, which is located fifteen miles west of Edinburgh. You can see the marble table, which has been restored to its rightful place back inside the house, along with Tam's haunted boots.

If you look closely at the table, you will see a distinctive semi-circular stain burnt into one corner of the marble. It just happens to be in the shape of a cloven hoof. Evidence perhaps, of the night that Tam angered the Devil.

THE GREEN LADY OF CRATHES CASTLE

Crathes Castle is a 16th century castle located in Aberdeenshire, built by the Burnetts of Leys. It's also the location of a ghostly sighting witnessed by Queen Victoria when visiting the castle.

The Queen claimed to have seen a child-like apparition alongside a green mist hovering in one of the castle's rooms. The ghosts lingered for a moment, before disappearing into the room's fireplace.

This was the beginning of several sightings of what became known as the Green Lady and her child. She would always appear in the same room and was often cradling a child in her arms. Eventually, after pacing back and forth, she would always disappear into the fireplace.

Locals believed that it was the restless spirit of a servant girl who was murdered by a member of the Burnett family after falling pregnant. It's said she was poisoned, killing both her and her unborn child, and this is why she appears as a green mist. Her true origins, though, remain shrouded in mystery.

Tales from the late 1500s say that Lady Agnes, following the Laird's death, developed an obsessive relationship with her son Alexander.

The freshly widowed Lady Agnes did not approve of her son being in a romantic relationship with a common girl called Bertha, so she poisoned his lover with deadly nightshade.

Alexander, upon discovering what his mother had done, was distraught. Lady Agnes died in mysterious circumstances shortly after her part in Bertha's death became known.

Was Alexander tormented enough to become a restless spirit wandering the castle? Is Lady Agnes haunting her former home? Or was Bertha the servant girl that locals suspected had been murdered for falling pregnant?

When renovation work took place at the castle in the 18th century, it's rumoured that they unearthed the skeletal remains of both a woman and a child. They had been buried beneath the very fireplace that the ghostly apparitions had disappeared into.

We may never know the identity of the Green Lady, but she has come to be known as a harbinger of doom for the Burnett family, perhaps as an act of vengeance from beyond the grave.

Other odd occurrences have also been noted at the castle, including unexplained noises coming from empty rooms and sudden cold chills experienced when walking through an otherwise warm room.

Brave visitors to Crathes Castle, which is now run by the National Trust of Scotland, speak of the sense of dread that washes over them when they are in the room where the apparition is said to appear.

This suggests that the ghost of the forlorn Green Lady and her child linger still.

ANNIE'S ROOM

Beneath the streets of Edinburgh lies a network of sixteenth and seventeenth century subterranean alleyways. A *close* is a Scots term for these old alleyways and a walk along The Royal Mile will reveal many of these narrow streets cutting through the city.

The Real Mary King's Close attraction is a cluster of underground passages named after one of its former residents, Mary King, an affluent merchant who lived there from around 1635.

The Close had become partially demolished in the name of progress and then buried as a city-beneath-the-city due to the building of the Royal Exchange in the 18th century.

The many tenement buildings within the Close rose high into the Edinburgh skyline and were considered by some to be the world's first skyscrapers. They housed people from all walks of life and social classes, crammed in tightly together, which became their downfall.

The mass of people living on top of each led to extremely unsanitary conditions. Numerous rodents made the Close their home and with them came the bubonic plague and the promise of a painful death.

In 1992, famed Japanese psychic Aiko Gibo visited the preserved Close while making a film about haunted places in Britain. There she made contact with the unhappy spirit of a young girl named Annie.

Aiko said that she could barely enter a room off Allan's Close due to the strength of emotions overwhelming her. Annie had approached her and gripped a tiny hand onto her trouser leg and conveyed her desire to go home and see her parents again.

According to the psychic, Annie's mother had abandoned her once she had begun exhibiting symptoms of the plague. Annie was also upset because she had lost her favourite doll. Aiko attempted to comfort Annie's spirit with the gift of a small doll, and since then hundreds of visitors have placed small toys and gifts in her room.

There are doll and toy donations from across the globe. First responders have left their badges out of respect to this little ghost girl. The original doll left by Aiko looked like a Barbie Doll but was actually part of the Daisy Doll airline collection designed by Mary Quant.

Once they have entered its depths, visitors to the Real Mary King's Close can view Annie's Room before they return to the surface. Aiko said that, as long as Annie's new doll remained in the room, then the spirit would be at peace.

However, on 17th April 2019, a guide at the Close made a shocking discovery – the doll was gone. A frantic search failed to find the doll again. To this day, the Real Mary King's Close is still appealing to the public to keep their eyes peeled in the search for Annie's doll. Somewhere out there, somebody has taken the one gift that comforted the lonely abandoned spirit of this little girl.

SKAILL HOUSE

Nestled on the shores of Mainland, the largest of the Orkney Islands, a mysterious house overlooks the magnificent Bay of Skaill.

Skaill House is a 17th century mansion that has been owned by the same family for 400 years. Originally built in 1620 by George Graham, the Bishop of Orkney, the house also overlooks the preserved Neolithic village of Skara Brae. Perhaps unknown to the original architect, the house was built on the remains of an ancient Pictish burial ground. This may explain some of the paranormal sightings and experiences reported by generations of lairds, employees and visitors passing through its rooms and hallways.

Many have heard strange footsteps creeping through the house when nobody else was there. Unusual sounds are often heard echoing through the house, unable to be located or easily identified by the modern listener, as if they come from another time or place.

Some have seen the ghost of an old lady wearing a shawl appear in doorways. Others have witnessed dogs barking at fleeting shadows and shapes that linger too long and have no source.

Today, the house is open to the public as a visitor attraction, with apartments for overnight stays. However, while undertaking restoration work to prepare the house for opening, fifteen Norse skeletons were unearthed near the south wing and beneath the east porch.

Previous work had discovered skeletal remains hidden beneath the main hall. The decision was made to not disturb the ancient graveyard any further, so each skeleton was carefully laid to rest again underneath the floors of Skaill House.

Could the spirits of those buried beneath the house still be making their presence felt?

Many of the ghostly experiences are actually attributed to a former resident of the house. The restless spirit, named Ubby, is believed to be the ghost of the man who created the small island in the middle of Skaill Loch.

Each day Ubby would row out to the centre of the loch with large rocks and stones. Once there, he would carefully drop them into the lake until he had created a little island. He then moved out of Skaill House and lived on the island he had created until the day he died there.

Perhaps preferring more company these days, Ubby appears to have taken up residence again in Skaill House. Unexplained cold spots, mysterious smells and apparitions of a tall male with dark hair are all attributed to Ubby's ghost.

You can rent Skaill House for a short break and immerse yourself in the history of the area, where Bronze and Iron Age discoveries have also been made.

And late at night, when the sounds of modern life have quietened down, you might just experience your own visit from the past.

THE HAUNTING OF CASTLE STUART

On the banks of the Moray Firth lies Castle Stuart, a 17th century tower house that is believed to be one of the most haunted castles in Scotland.

When the Earl of Moray inherited the castle, he decided to rent it out, but soon discovered that people were too afraid to stay within its walls.

There were whispered rumours from employees and locals of headless ghosts wandering the corridors, terrible screams from an unknown source and footsteps running up and down the stairs at night.

His solution? To offer a reward to any brave soul who dared spend an entire night in the castle. Alas, the Earl discovered that there were very few who were willing to take the risk, given the castle's chilling reputation.

Eventually, the reward drew the interest of four local men, a minister, a Presbyterian church elder, a shoemaker and a large, strong man called Rob Angus, who prided himself on not being afraid of anything.

The Earl had his servants set up two chairs, a table with a brass lamp, a mirror and a bookcase in the most haunted of the rooms, and then invited each of the men to spend a night there.

The minister took the first turn to be locked in the room, relaxing in one of the chairs until he drifted off to sleep. Unfortunately, he had a terrifying nightmare of a large man covered in blood slowly entering the room and sitting down in the chair beside him. Upon waking he found that he was still alone, but his mind was never the same and he didn't wish to claim his reward.

The church elder arrived on the second night armed with his bible. After being locked in the room, he stayed up reading as the hours ticked by. Suddenly, an enormous blood-soaked man burst into the room and a skull appeared in the mirror sporting a manic grin.

As the large man charged at him with a dagger, the church elder was overcome by fear and fainted. He was discovered by servants the following morning and his traumatic experience haunted him for a long time, so he too declined to claim the reward.

The third night saw the nervous shoemaker arrive, ready to be locked inside the haunted room. He settled himself near to the fire and clasped his hands in prayer, in the hope that it might protect him from whatever evil lay within the castle walls.

Deep into the night, he was startled by the creak of the door opening. The terrified shoemaker spun around to see a menacing dark creature with cloven hooves advancing towards him.

The shoemaker fainted as the creature leapt towards him, leaving the servants to discover him unconscious on the floor the following morning. He was as equally disinterested in claiming the reward as the minister and church elder had been before him.

The fourth night saw big Rob Angus step into the house and declare that there was nothing in this world he feared. He happened to be friends with one of the servants and the two of them spent some time drinking whisky together before Rob was taken upstairs to spend the night in the haunted room.

"See you in the morning, Rob," said the servant.
"You will find me as I am, or dead," Rob replied.

And that was the last time Rob was seen alive.

When the servant unlocked the door to the haunted room the next day, he entered a scene of devastation. The mirror lay smashed on the floor and every bit of furniture was scattered about the room, broken beyond repair.

And Rob Angus was missing.

The servant rushed to the broken window and stared down at the ground. There, amongst the shattered glass, lay the cut and bruised body of Rob. The servant presumed that he had fallen to his death, but could not tell if he had leapt from the window of his own accord, or had been thrown through it by an unknown assailant.

However, there was an eye witness to the event.

A local farmer had been herding his sheep past Castle Stuart by the light of the full moon when he glanced up to see a glow coming from within one of the castle's rooms. At the same time, crashing sounds and a terrible scream rang out into the night, before the window suddenly burst outwards and he saw the body of a large man fall to the ground with a heavy thud.

The petrified farmer looked up at the gaping hole where the window had been and was greeted by a twisted grinning face staring back down at him. Until his death, the farmer told all who would listen that he had looked into the face of the Devil that night.

So the Earl of Moray's challenge was failed by all who attempted it, but the terrifying tales surrounding Castle Stuart did not end there.

In 1798, a wild storm swept in off the Moray Firth and battered the castle, ripping the roof off the East Tower. With the main part of the castle now exposed to the elements, the decision was made to simply seal off the damaged wing.

So the haunted room inside the East Tower was walled off from the rest of the castle, and there it lay neglected in the darkness for over 130 years.

Until one fateful night in the 1930s, when a Canadian man named John Cameron learned why sometimes it's better to leave mysterious boarded-up parts of an old castle alone.

John and his team of workers were carrying out repairs on the castle. Being a hardworking man, John had stayed late at the castle to continue a job, long after his colleagues had gone home for the evening.

He was all alone when he noticed that a particular patch of plaster appeared different to the rest. Climbing a ladder, he chiselled away at the plaster, unknowingly opening up the old East Tower.

With one final blow, his chisel broke through the sealed wall and he peered into the darkness beyond, revealing the edges of long-abandoned steps that used to carry servants and challengers up to the haunted room.

At that exact moment, John froze with terror as a sudden rush of air carried a loud strangled cry from the depths of the darkened tower.

His breath came in shallow gasps and his heart thundered in his chest as he told himself that it must have simply been a pocket of air or gas escaping, the noise distorted by the empty staircase beyond.

Hands shaking, he slowly raised his tools and struck another piece of the plaster away. He cried out as an invisible force struck his chest and flung him backwards, his arms flailing as he fell from the ladder and hit the ground hard.

He lifted himself and fled from the castle as his nose and lungs filled with the putrid stench of rot and decay.

Once outside, he took a moment to calm himself down and regain his senses. Logically, he knew he would have to re-enter the castle to gather his tools and turn off all the temporary electric lights he had set up.

Gathering his wits and his courage, John turned on his car engine and angled the headlights so that they provided a light source through the open door and into the castle. This would enable him to find his way back out in the dark, once he had switched off the temporary lights.

With a set jaw and determined stride, he made his way back inside the now eerily quiet castle. Gaining in confidence, he picked up his tools and switched off the lights.

He found himself plunged into darkness, the headlights nowhere to be found. He reached his arm out and felt his way towards the door, realising that it had somehow closed behind him since he had re-entered the castle.

As his hand gripped the door handle, he felt icy fingers grasp his shoulders and attempt to drag him back into the darkened depths of the castle.

Screaming, he flung himself at the door, yanked it open and burst into the bright beams of his headlights.

From that moment onwards, he vowed never to enter Castle Stuart ever again.

Now a luxury hotel and golf resort, Castle Stuart is a place steeped in history. Only a short drive from Inverness, the castle has eight bedrooms available for an overnight stay. Generally popular with golfers, the castle may also attract those who wish to rise to the Earl of Moray's challenge, daring themselves to stay a night within the castle.

THE GHOST OF ACKERGILL TOWER

Ackergill Tower was a prestigious castle hotel in Wick, in the Highlands of Scotland. Formerly described as one of the most luxurious hotels in the world, the castle is now a privately-owned estate. The castle and its grounds have also been at the centre of many bloody feuds throughout history.

The castle was formerly owned by the Keith family, the lands of Ackergill having been inherited by John Keith of Inverugie in 1354 from the Cheynes family.

The first mention of the castle's existence was in 1538. A legend from the time tells that the Keith Clan was feuding with the Gunn Clan, which resulted in many attacks and murders on both sides.

It's said that the Keith family kidnapped Helen Gunn, a woman known for her outstanding beauty. However, she had no interest in her abductor's advances and would not tolerate being kept against her will.

While being held in a room at the top of the castle, Helen fell, or jumped, from a window while trying to escape. Unfortunately, this resulted in her death and escalated the bad blood between the feuding clans.

The legend goes that the spirit of Helen Gunn lingers still and is often seen as an apparition with long black hair, wearing a red ball gown. Other sightings tell of her appearing at the castle as a green lady.

Helen's death led to the Battle of Champions, a judicial combat between the Gunns and Keiths. The duel was held at the chapel of St Tear (or Tayre), just east of the village, and resulted in the massacre of the Gunn Clan.

The castle continued to attract feudal attention and in 1547 the Sinclairs of Girnigoe seized the castle, before Mary of Guise, who was the Regent of Scotland at the time, ordered it be returned to the Keith family. In 1549, she appointed Laurence Oliphant as keeper of Ackergill.

However, the determined Sinclairs attacked and seized the castle again, leading to it changing ownership several times over the years. In 1612, the Sinclairs tried a different tactic and purchased the castle legally. They then sold the castle to the Dunbars, who built a number of extensions to the building.

It became a hotel after being sold in 1986 and undergoing two years of extensive renovations, before finally being opened to the public. While it is no longer possible to stay at Ackergill Tower, there are those who have visited the room where Helen Gunn was supposedly held captive. My friend, Rebecca Loughlin, was one of those fortunate enough to visit before it became a private estate.

Rebecca says *"I was there a few times before it was sold and I have been inside the lady's room at the top of the tower. The décor was in a vintage style, with a large bed. I never saw the ghost of the lady, but what I do remember most is that the room was always unnaturally cold, even on hot days in the middle of summer"*.

CATHEDRAL HOUSE HOTEL

Cathedral House Hotel is a beautiful 19th century baronial-style boutique hotel and restaurant situated a short walk from Glasgow Cathedral. With infamous origins, it's also believed to be one of the most haunted buildings in Glasgow.

In 1877, Cathedral House was built as a halfway house for prisoners returning to society from the neighbouring Duke Street Prison. The prison housed some of the most notorious criminals in the whole of Scotland and was known for having appalling living conditions for its inmates.

Demolished in 1958, the only physical remains of Duke Street Prison is the boundary wall behind Cathedral House Hotel. However, beyond the physical realm, the former inmates of this historical prison are said to still be making their presence felt.

Many criminals were executed at the prison, with twelve of those executions carried out in the 20th century. Susan Newell, an inmate found guilty of strangling a paperboy, was the last woman to be executed in Scotland. She was hanged at the prison in October 1923.

Many believe this to be the reason for the numerous paranormal sightings that people have experienced within the hotel. The most common of these is feeling an invisible presence brush against you while walking on the stairs.

Other stories tell of the sound of two children playing on the top floor when there are no children present. There have even been eye-witness accounts of furniture moving itself around within the rooms.

Could these experiences be the spirits of former prisoners? Upon closer examination, there may be an alternative reason for these ghostly occurrences.

Directly across from Cathedral House Hotel lies the Glasgow Necropolis and many of its bedrooms look out upon this large cemetery, which itself is said to be haunted.

In 1933, three people killed in a tragic tramcar accident were buried within the Necropolis, with a statue of a woman sitting guard atop their grave. It's said that statue turns its head to watch visitors as they make their way through the graveyard. Perhaps she sometimes turns her attention towards the hotel.

Ghost hunting groups have been drawn to the hotel to conduct their paranormal investigations. Many of these have resulted in unusual orbs and other oddities being captured in photos and video recordings, as well as unusual electromagnetic field (EMF) and trifield readings.

The investigations have also claimed to have recorded a chair moving on its own and unexplained voices. Is this evidence of the paranormal experiences previously reported? There are many similarities. And if you have the courage, you can book yourself on one of the ghost tours that explore the Necropolis and culminates with a night spent trying to contact the spirits within the hotel.

CHAPTER 2

TERRIFYING TRAVELS

Driving through the gorgeous Scottish countryside, it's hard to feel anything except a sense of peace and wellbeing. However, beneath this beauty may hide a more frightening experience for the unwary traveller.

As sunlight filters through the canopy, you feel a cool breeze on the forest air. The ancient trees hold a deep wisdom, having bore silent witness to man's events throughout history. And now, they are watching you.

This chapter reminds us that even when we are travelling in the most wild and isolated parts of Scotland, we may not be as alone as we think we are.

SCOTLAND'S MOST HAUNTED ROAD

The scenic South West Coastal 300 route takes you around some of the most beautiful parts of Scotland. Its southern arm leads you along wide stretches of the A75, a road that has for many decades been the site of supernatural occurrences.

The ninety-three miles of road cuts through Dumfries & Galloway, an excellent shortcut inland from the West coast, but you won't find many delivery drivers on its route. This is because the A75 Kinmount straight, stretching between Carrutherstown and Annan, is believed to be the most haunted highway in Scotland.

In 1962, two brothers, Derek and Norman Ferguson, experienced a horrific incident on the highway. They claimed to have witnessed a mysterious out-of-control furniture van swerving across the road, followed by wild animals leaping at their windshield.

They had been on a road trip around Scotland in their father's car and were fifteen miles away from their home in Annan when their journey took a terrifying turn.

It began with a hen launching itself at their window and culminated in great cats bounding towards their vehicle. They claimed a mysterious presence had tried to take control of their steering wheel.

A great wind whipped up and buffeted the car as it attempted to force them to hit the animals and odd creatures that littered the road ahead.

Strange screams and crazy cackles rang out around them as they slid and swerved their way through the sudden crowd. Apparently, an old woman was seen frantically waving her hands as she headed towards the windscreen, closely followed by a long-haired screaming man. The pair were soon lost in a menagerie of chickens, goats, dogs and even more strange and exotic creatures.

The brother's relief at spotting a furniture van was short-lived when they realised that it too was a spectre… and they were about to crash into it.

Fortunately, they managed to stay on the road and lived to tell the tale, though both brothers became ill from the violent shaking of their vehicle during the traumatic experience.

When they pulled over and stopped, everything disappeared before their eyes. There was no sign of the van or animals.

They were all alone.

This spooky incident of the two brothers is in addition to numerous reports of screaming hags, ghostly figures crossing the road and UFO sightings in the area.

It's no wonder then that lorry drivers have learned to avoid this route. Over the years locals claim to have seen many traumatised drivers who had chosen to sleep over in the lay-bys along its route. Visibly shaken, their tales told of nights disturbed by all manner of phantoms and creatures.

Individuals who did not work for the same lorry firm, and had never met, recounted chillingly similar tales of dishevelled people carrying mysterious bundles and pulling rickety handcarts that creaked past them in the night.

They had lain frozen in fear as they watched the long line of phantoms trickle by, close enough to hear their laboured breathing and make out the details of their faces through the window.

These ghostly parades were a common sighting, leading some paranormal experts to suggest they were the lost souls of those who followed the war camps into battle, doomed to march forever.

They say an army marches on its stomach, and many animals were herded along with the soldiers. This may explain why ghostly animals sometimes get loose and seemingly attack drivers along this route.

It fails to explain, though, the numerous accounts of drivers who believe they have run over a person emerging from the dark at the edge of the road.

Drivers have testified that a figure runs into their path, giving them no time to swerve. They have hit the figure, heard the bang, felt the bump... but when they stopped and got out to check, the body was gone.

The first record of ghostly sightings on the road seemed to have occurred in 1957 when a lorry driver reported that he had hit a couple who had been walking along the road.

Upon inspection, the couple had disappeared. Their bodies vanished as if they had never been there. Yet the incident was real enough for the lorry driver to hand himself in to police.

Over the years, there have been many instances of witnesses stating that they had seen the couple. There's something uncanny about the way that their descriptions of the couple matched each other, despite the years between sightings.

Linked arm-in-arm, the couple walk along the road dressed in Victorian-era attire and are easily recognisable due to the fact that the gentleman is missing his eyes.

In 1995, an unfortunate couple experienced a different figure haunting the route.

Garston and Monica Miller were driving home when a man suddenly appeared in front of their car. His bedraggled form wore only an old hessian sack and his extended arm held out a rag that he pointed towards the couple's car.

Like many before them, they believed they had struck the man and, despite being unable to find a body, went straight to the Annan police to report the accident. Their search found nothing.

Unsurprisingly, the road has a terrible record for car accidents and is avoided by locals at night. Perhaps if you travel along this route enough times, you might just have your own tale of ghostly encounters to tell.

THE GHILLIE DHU

Clad in an outfit of moss and leaves, the Ghillie Dhu guards its forest home. A lone male faerie with wild dark hair, it's said he inhabits the birch forests of Gairloch in Wester Ross, a village in the North-West Highlands.

The village is a popular tourist destination on the North Coast 500 route. But if you linger too long amongst these trees, you might just find more than you bargained for.

The Ghillie Dhu (or Gillie Dubh), translated from Scottish Gaelic as *dark-haired lad*, is generally a shy creature, choosing to avoid contact with adult humans unless they stray from the path and invade the glades and groves of its forest home. It then becomes aggressive towards these trespassers.

However, in contrast to its fearsome dislike for adults, it is known to be a kind and gentle creature towards children.

Legend tells that in the late 18th century a young girl from the village became lost in the woods. Tired and afraid, Jessie Macrae was found by the Ghillie Dhu.

The faerie comforted her during the night, keeping her protected and warm, before leading her through his forest home to safety the following morning.

Despite this kind-hearted gesture, the local landowner, Sir Hector Mackenzie of Gairloch, and a group of Mackenzie dignitaries attempted to hunt and capture the creature.

The team of five men set off with guns one evening and hunted through the night, but could not find the faerie.

The Ghillie Dhu had been sighted by many people over a forty year period. However, Jessie was the only person that he ever spoke to.

After the failed hunt, it's said that the Ghillie Dhu was never seen again. This has led some to speculate that it wasn't a nature spirit, but was instead a human being with a medical condition.

The small stature of the creature suggests a form of dwarfism, with his outfit gathered from his surroundings after making his home in the woods.

This would explain why he avoided the adults of the time, who were less understanding of his condition, but was kind to children. After being hunted, he may have decided to move to safety within quieter woods.

It may also explain why he was sighted within the time period of an adult human life span but then disappeared.

Whether spirit or human, all the Ghillie Dhu wanted was to be left alone to live in peace.

The ghillie suit, an item of camouflage clothing that allows the wearer to blend into foliage through the use of twigs and leaves (often worn by snipers on military operations), gets its name from this Scottish urban legend.

THE OLD MAN OF STORR

If you take a trip to the Isle of Skye, you may happen upon the Old Man of Storr. This rocky pinnacle has a grassy slope one side and a steep rocky face on the other, towering over western Skye.

Legend tells that this pinnacle was formed when a giant, who lived in Trotternish Ridge, was buried in the ground and his thumb was left protruding from the earth.

A hike up to the rocks that surround the Old Man rewards adventurous travellers with beautiful views of the water and surrounding mainland.

Though an alternative legend behind the origins of the Old Man suggests you may need to keep your eyes peeled for a mythical Scottish creature.

It's said that a hobgoblin-like creature called a brownie was actually the true architect of the pinnacle. Brownies are known to befriend human families and can often be coerced into doing good deeds.

A villager from Skye called O'Sheen supposedly saved the life of a brownie who dwelled on the island. He and the grateful brownie then became friends.

Tragically, O'Sheen's wife passed away and he died not long after from a broken heart. The brownie, pained by the loss of his friend, decided to create a memorial in his honour. He chiselled out two rocky pinnacles, one to remember O'Sheen and the other dedicated to his wife.

MACKINNON'S CAVE

MacKinnon's Cave on the Isle of Mull in the Inner Hebrides is fascinating from both a mythical and adventurous perspective.

Travellers who dare to cross the muddy ground and large boulder to reach its entrance will find one of the deepest caves in the Hebrides. It's also the longest sea cave on the west coast of Scotland.

Legend says it was here that Abbot MacKinnon, who gave his name to the cave, spent time hidden there in the 15th century in order to avoid capture by the MacLean Clan.

Inside the cave, which is only accessible between half and low tide, a torch will reveal a large, flat slab of rock. This is known as Fingal's Table and it's believed to have been used as an altar by earlier followers of Christianity.

In 1773, Dr Samuel Johnson and James Boswell visited MacKinnon's Cave. They decided to measure the dimensions of the cave using only a walking stick.

If they were thorough in their mapping of the cave, they would have discovered a tunnel that connects it with the nearby Cormorant Cave. Which may explain the mysterious disappearance of a local piper who tried to beat the fairies in a piping competition. Apparently, he walked into the cave with his dog but was never seen again. After a while, his dog returned crazed and hairless. So, travellers beware if you are visiting this legendary cave for yourself.

FINGAL'S CAVE

The uninhabited island of Staffa, in the Inner Hebrides, is home to one of the strangest looking caves in the world. Fingal's Cave is a 227ft cavern formed entirely (and uniquely) of hexagonal-shaped basalt columns, similar to the shape and structure of the famous Giant's Causeway in Northern Ireland.

One unlikely legend that surrounds Fingal's Cave is that it was named after an Irish giant named Fionn mac Cumhaill (alternatively Finn McCool) who was tired of getting his feet wet as he traversed the Irish Sea, so he built the Giant's Causeway between County Antrim and Scotland.

However, while creating the bridge, he learns that one of his most feared enemies, the Scottish giant Benandonner, is on his way to fight him.

Knowing he cannot possibly match the strength of his fearsome opponent, Fionn's wife, Oona, disguises him as a baby and hides him in a cradle.

Oona then bakes some delicious cakes, secretly hiding lumps of iron inside some of them. Benandonner storms into the house in search of Fionn, but cannot find him anywhere, so decides to wait.

Oona offers him a cake and when the giant bites into it he roars in pain as he chips his teeth on the hidden iron. Oona immediately bursts into laughter, ridiculing Benandonner for being soft and weak, stating that her husband regularly eats those cakes with no issues.

She then proceeds to feed one of them (with no hidden iron) to her baby (the disguised Fionn).

Upon witnessing this, Benandonner decides he doesn't want to meet the father of such a strong baby, so returns to Scotland, breaking up the causeway as he goes, so that Fionn cannot hunt him down.

Whilst we can reasonably say it probably wasn't the work of giants, the cave certainly has uniquely odd features that have no doubt added to its mystique.

The cave has excellent natural acoustics, which has given rise to a different legend about the origins of its name. James Macpherson, an 18th century Scots poet, gained fame as the '*translator*' of the Ossian cycle of epic poems. And he may have coincidentally identified a legendary hero for whom the cave was named.

In 1761 he published the lengthily-named *Fingal, an Ancient Epic Poem in Six Books, together with Several Other Poems composed by Ossian, the Son of Fingal.*

Some say the cave was named after this epic hero in 1772 (at the height of Macpherson's fame) by Sir Joseph Banks. Before that, the cave was called '*An Uamh Bhin*' or '*The Melodious Cave*' in Gaelic.

However, it's believed that the name Fingal or Fionnghall means '*white stranger*' and that in old Gaelic this would appear as Finn.

This is in line with another legend which suggests the cave was named after an Irish general called Finn MacCumhaill.

Finn (or Fingal) MacCumhaill was believed to have been the father of Ossian, traditional bard of the Gaels. Finn and his band of followers can be thought of as being similar in nature to King Arthur and the Knights of the Round Table, but with a Celtic twist.

Finn became famous across Scotland due to his deeds being immortalised in Ossianic heroic verse by the Gaels who had come across from Ireland. A hero of song would be the perfect choice for this naturally melodic cave.

In 1829, composer Felix Mendelssohn wrote an overture called The Hebrides, which was also known as Fingal's Cave overture as it was inspired by the echoes he heard when visiting the cave.

In more modern verse, Pink Floyd wrote an instrumental song called *Fingal's Cave*. In 1999, the Scottish Celtic rock band Wolfstone released their album entitled *Seven*, which also contained an instrumental track called *Fingal's Cave*.

Those interested in the history of the cave may wish to pay a visit to Lloyd House at the California Institute of Technology, which boasts both a mural depicting the cave and a wooden statue named Fingal, one of its oldest and most precious heirlooms.

We may never know how it truly got its name, but there's no doubting that this unique cave is worth a visit to hear these strange and inspiring acoustics for yourself.

CORRYVRECKAN WHIRLPOOL

Between the islands of Jura and Scarba, off the west coast of Scotland, unusual underwater topography and speeding currents combine to create amazing effects on the surface.

This phenomenon has also been attributed to Cailleach Bheur, the hag goddess of winter, who it's said uses this area to wash her great plaid. The swirling roar of her washing can be heard twenty miles away and lasts for three days.

This washing ritual signals the changing of the seasons from autumn to winter. Once she has finished, the plaid is pure white, which she then lays across the land as a blanket of snow.

This is why the Gulf of Corryvreckan is named from the Gaelic '*Coire Bhreacain*' which means '*cauldron of the plaid*' or '*cauldron of the speckled seas*'.

Scottish author and photographer, Alasdair Alpin MacGregor, said that the Cailleach occupying the whirlpool was '*the fiercest of the Highland storm kelpies*'.

Scottish poet and novelist Charles Mackay wrote a poem called *The Kelpie of Corrievreckan* in which a young woman leaves her lover for a sea kelpie. However, once she has departed with the creature she discovers that the kelpie lives at the bottom of the sea.

Somewhat inevitably, she drowns.

In another legend, there was a Norse king called Breacan who wanted to win the hand of a local princess, but her father insisted that he pass a trial first.

To test his bravery and suitability for marriage, Breacan was tasked with mooring his boat beside the whirlpool for three days and three nights.

To aid him, Breacan commissioned three ropes to be made. The first was made from wool, the second from hemp, and the third was woven from a maiden's hair, whose purity would ensure that the rope was unbreakable.

Legend says that on the first night the hemp rope broke, the wool rope snapped on the second night, and the rope made from maiden's hair broke on the third night.

This resulted in the unfortunate Breacan dying when the boat was dragged beneath the waves.

A surviving crew member recovered the body and, upon seeing this, the maiden who had supplied the hair guiltily admitted that she was not as pure as she made out.

Nowadays, the turbulent waters have made Corryvreckan the third-largest whirlpool in the world, with waves that can soar over 30ft into the air. It's said that you can hear the roar of the churning maelstrom from over ten miles away.

And if you close your eyes on a crisp autumn evening, you can imagine the Cailleach washing her great plaid, signalling the coming of winter.

AM FEAR LIATH MÒR

High on the summit of Ben Macdui, the second-highest mountain in Scotland (and the highest in the Cairngorms National Park), lives a mysterious creature called Am Fear Liath Mòr, the Gaelic name for the more commonly known Big Grey Man.

Many hikers who have traversed the mountain's 4,295 feet have returned with terrifying tales of encounters with a huge dark presence, either seen or felt, that followed them across the mountain.

Those who have laid eyes upon the Big Grey Man have described a large creature around ten feet tall, with broad shoulders, long arms and short hair covering most of his body. He is often seen waving his arms as if shooing the hikers off his mountain.

His presence is often felt as a dark dread, letting adventurers know that they are trespassing in his territory and are not welcome there.

There have been reported sighting of the Big Grey Man dating back centuries, but it wasn't until a respected professor recounted his terrifying experience that the legend of Am Fear Liath Mòr was truly born.

In 1891, Professor Norman Collie, an experienced mountaineer, claimed he met the dark presence while descending from the mountain. In 1925, he told his tale to members of the Cairngorm Club.

Professor Collie described walking back down the mountain in a thick mist when he noticed that his footsteps weren't the only ones descending the mountain.

Every few steps, his own stride was matched by the crunch of an unseen presence, slowly following behind him. The timing of the mysterious crunch suggested a stride length three to four times larger than his own.

Believing that it was just a coincidence or his imagination, he took a few more steps, then waited. The crunch came again, louder this time, as if the unknown follower was catching up.

He scanned the area around him, but the mist hid the details. Gripped with terror, Professor Collie set off again at pace, hurriedly bounding over miles of boulders until he reached the relative safety of Rothiemurchus Forest. He swore never to return to the summit of Ben Macdui by himself ever again.

His tale contains many similarities to other encounters with the Big Grey Man. In 1943, Alexander Tewnion was descending the mountain via the Coire Etchachan path, when he noticed he was being suddenly being approached at speed by a large shadow-like form.

The form brought with it a sense of danger so overwhelming that Alexander grabbed his pistol and fired three shots at the shape, before escaping towards Glen Derry. He believes he wounded and scared off whatever was following him that day.

The most common theme from experiences with the Big Grey Man is that of a pervasive sense of fear and dread causing many climbers to panic. This eerie feeling is usually a precursor to many strange sounds, including footsteps, following hikers and climbers as they make their way down Ben Macdui.

The Big Grey Man appears to have a favoured hunting ground, with the majority of reports stating that they were followed in an area known as Lairig Ghru Pass. Some have claimed that, when the sense of dread hits them, it's accompanied by a sudden urge to leap over the cliff edge at Lurcher's Crag. Many believe this to be an evil power, and goal, of the mysterious creature stalking them. And those that do make it to safety are left with the lingering feeling that they should never return.

Like most urban legends, science has attempted to explain these mysterious sightings. Their best suggestion, proposed by Johann Silberschlag in 1780, is a phenomenon called Brocken Spectre (also called Brocken Bow or Mountain Spectre), which is caused by the human eye being tricked by an optical illusion into thinking that a huge shadow-like shape is facing them. In reality, it's the sun distorting their own shadow across a misty or cloudy area, misinterpreted by the human eye and mind. This phenomenon has also been shown to be effective from inside aircraft in the same conditions.

However, this is of little comfort to those wishing to climb Ben Macdui, because whether it is created by the human mind, or is, in reality, a mythical creature, the sense of terror that the Big Grey Man brings is still the same.

GLASGOW'S HAUNTED ARCHES

Glasgow's Arches was formerly a derelict area underneath Glasgow Central Train Station. Over the years it has had many purposes, including becoming a nightclub. However, it is also an area known for ghostly experiences.

The first apparition that haunts Glasgow's Arches is thought to be the spirit of a young girl, who has frequently been sighted roaming the corridors.

In 2009, during the Alien Wars run, many actors participating in the event claimed to have repeatedly seen the ghost a young girl. They described her as being dressed in vintage-looking clothing and said she would drift along the ground, darting between different corridors. The girl is often described as looking lost as if she is requiring assistance, but when those who have seen her move too close, she lets out an ear-piercing scream and disappears.

The second apparition relates to a paranormal experience that is often heard, but yet to be seen. Prior to the rejuvenation of the Arches, the area was frequented by prostitutes and citizens with nefarious schemes.

One night, a prostitute was brutally murdered and her body was stuffed inside a stairwell in an empty building, which would later become the newly renovated Arches. They say that the stairwell was then sealed off with bricks and cement, without her body ever being discovered. And on a quiet night, you can still hear her muffled screams echoing through the Arches.

DUMBARTON'S DOG SUICIDE BRIDGE

The ornate Victorian Overtoun Bridge in Dumbarton, built in 1895, has acquired a peculiar reputation for being the site of many attempted suicides, by dogs wishing to leap from the top.

It's said that normal dog walks have quickly turned into a terrifying experience as the poor animals have seemingly been willed to jump from the highest point of the bridge, injuring or killing themselves in the process.

Witnesses have stated that their animals often freeze before rushing up the bridge as if they have sensed or been overcome by a strange malevolent energy or presence that only they can see.

There have been reports of this happening to hundreds of dogs since the 1950s. Unfortunately, many have ended up so severely injured that they have passed away on the jagged rocks protruding from the steep valley bed 50 feet beneath the bridge.

Locals now called the bridge 'dog suicide bridge' and many refuse to walk their own dogs near it.

The strangest aspect of all is that many panic-stricken dog owners have rushed down the valley in search of their pet, only to discover that their dog is whimpering and severely injured… but is trying to climb back up to the top of the bridge, so that they can leap off again. They refuse to answer to their owners and appear still possessed by the compulsion to complete their suicidal task.

Some have tried to explain the mystery in terms of geographical terrain, suggesting that the dogs become over-stimulated by wild animal scents in the area, blindly following them with disastrous consequences.

However, it's the terrain itself that may also offer a clue to a more mystical explanation.

The bridge is located within a luscious quiet area that matches descriptions of 'thin places' described by pagan Celts as being an enthralling point where the barrier between heaven and Earth is at its thinnest.

The mystery has inspired books and TV episodes but has yet to be solved. The locals are convinced that it is a ghost possessing the animals, possibly the 'White Lady of Overtoun'.

The story goes that the White Lady of Overtoun is the spirit of a grieving widow, whose husband, John White, passed away in 1908.

Many local residents have claimed to have seen or felt the White Lady, spotting her staring back at them in windows, or wandering around forlornly.

If you wish to explore the area for yourself, remember that the depth of the gorge is deceptive when you are standing in the middle of the bridge.

Also, maybe leave your dog at home for this one.

SCOTLAND'S STANDING STONES

Scotland has a number of standing stones dotted around the country, some of which date back to the country's very first settlers, over 10,000 years ago.

But why did they erect these monuments? What purpose, normal or mystical, did they serve?

On the west coast of the Isle of Lewis, the Calanais Standing Stones are a cross-shaped arrangement of stones believed to have been placed there over 5,000 years ago.

Also known as Fir Bhreig, which means 'false men' in Gaelic, the stones have been the subject of several myths and legends. Most popular among these is the belief that the stones are the petrified souls of giants who refused to convert to Christianity. It's also believed that once a year, on the dawn of the Midsummer Solstice, a spectre can be seen wandering around the stones.

In Orkney, there lies a Neolithic henge and a near-perfect stone circle known as the Ring of Brodgar. It's suggested that these were once a temple, important to the theological beliefs of Scandinavian invaders from the 9th century. In modern times, crowds have waited patiently at the site for UFOs to appear.

Machrie Moor, on the Isle of Arran, is formed of six stone circles. Legend states that a group of fairies gathered at the top of the mountain, Durra-na-each, and flicked pebbles into the moor below, creating the circles we see today. Their true purpose, however, remains unknown.

CHAPTER 3

DISTURBING THE DEAD

Disturbing the eternal peace of those who have crossed over to the other side rarely ends well. Whether that's deliberately violating their final resting place, or accidentally trespassing upon the grounds in which their ghosts still linger.

Such spirits can often be harbingers of doom, or simply reliving the battles they fought in life.

This chapter unearths tales of strange coffins, displaced spirits and people who lived violent lives. And once their slumber has been disturbed, their malevolence continues from beyond the grave.

THE ARTHUR'S SEAT COFFINS

The year is 1836. You are an Edinburgh schoolboy, innocently hunting rabbits with two of your friends on a warm summer evening when you make a macabre discovery. Seventeen miniature coffins, carved by an unknown hand and hidden behind three-pointed slabs of stone inside a small cave on the north-eastern face of Arthur's Seat.

Each of these coffins holds a small human effigy with intricately formed bodies and expressively painted faces. Each occupant has been carved from a single piece of solid wood.

The unknown creator has even sewn miniature clothes and shoes to put on their carved bodies. They were arranged in the cave in three tiers, two rows of eight and a solitary coffin on top.

On 20th July 1836, the *London Times* reported that the first tier of coffins had decayed quite badly, the clothes becoming mouldy. In the second tier, the effects of ageing had not been so prominent. The final coffin had looked quite recent when discovered.

It's not known when these figures were made, but some of them were already decaying when they were found, suggesting that they had been created over a number of years. The main questions on everybody's lips though are why were they made? What purpose did they serve? Why were they secreted away inside this cave?

Some declared them evil and stated that they must have been used for witchcraft rituals and other dark purposes. In an article published on 16th July 1836, *The Scotsman* newspaper declared it a 'Satanic spell-manufactory!'.

Others suggest they may have simply been a morbid way to commemorate the victims of Edinburgh's most infamous murderers, Burke and Hare.

Over a period of about ten months in 1828, the duo would stalk the streets of Edinburgh in search of victims. They would sell the corpses to local anatomist and physician Robert Knox, whose questionable morals allowed him to turn a blind eye to where the cadavers for his experiments and research came from.

Did the creator of the Arthur's Seat coffins intend to honour the victims of Burke and Hare?

And if so, why were Burke and Hare found guilty of sixteen murders, but there were seventeen coffins?

Did the carver know something the authorities never discovered? Was the solitary coffin on its own an acknowledgement of the missing murder?

More likely, it may have been a nod to the accidental manner in which Burke and Hare began their murder spree. A lodger in Hare's house had died. Rather than go through the usual channels, the pair decided to sell the body to Knox and received £7 10s, a fantastic sum for two Irish labourers.

A short while later another female lodger was suffering from a fever, which Hare believed would deter other potential lodgers from staying at his house. This proved to be the beginning of their notoriety.

Together, they murdered her and sold the body. And so it continued until they were eventually caught when other lodgers discovered the body of their final victim and contacted the police.

One lodger dead of natural causes, plus sixteen murdered. A solitary coffin placed on its own, sixteen placed in rows. The similarity between the murders and the coffins is obvious, but is it just a coincidence?

All seventeen real-life bodies were dissected, thus never receiving a proper burial. But had their spirits received the decent burial they deserved within those tiny coffins hidden on an Edinburgh hillside?

If so, then why were all 17 of the figures dressed exclusively in male clothing, when twelve of Burke and Hare's victims were female?

Honorific burial or macabre witchcraft? To decide for yourself, head along to the National Museum of Scotland in Edinburgh. Only eight coffins endured the years, the other nine being lost to time.

Or if you are feeling brave, take a trip through the Edinburgh Dungeon to experience being stalked by Burke and Hare.

Before we move on to the next urban legend, I shall leave you with one final twist in this strange tale.

In 1906 *The Scotsman* newspaper reported a story told to them by a local woman. Her father owned business premises that were sometimes frequented by what she described as a 'daft man'.

She went on to recount how this 'daft man' had once shown her father a piece of paper upon which he had drawn three small coffins. Each of the images contained a date below them of 1837, 1838 and 1840.

The Scotsman goes on to explain that the woman's father had been dismissive of the man.

However, in 1837 a near relative of her father passed away, in 1838 his cousin died, and then in 1840 his brother also died. The dates of their deaths matched the dates below the hand-drawn coffins he had been shown that day.

Following the funeral in 1840, the same 'daft man', who turned out to be a deaf mute, once again visited the business premises. This time he simply glowered at the woman's father, before vanishing, never to be seen again.

Was this mysterious man the creator of the coffins? Had the woman's father somehow angered somebody who controlled occult powers? Were the predicted deaths his vengeance? These are just some of the questions that remain unanswered to this day.

THE MACKENZIE POLTERGEIST

We remain in Edinburgh for this next unexplained tale as we visit a resident of Greyfriars Kirkyard. The long-deceased Sir George Mackenzie has a reputation for being an extremely aggressive poltergeist.

In the 17th century, the draconian lawyer earned the nickname *Bluidy Mackenzie* for his part in the ruthless torture of those who opposed King Charles II's religious reforms.

Bluidy Mackenzie would bring the captives to a secluded corner of Greyfriars Kirkyard where he would proceed to painfully torture them, allowing the guards to do the same.

The imprisoned souls would then be decapitated and their heads stuck onto the spiked gate. And they were the lucky ones. Many others were simply left without food or water to die slowly, all while being mocked and jeered by the monstrously jubilant face of *Bluidy Mackenzie.*

A violent man in life and now a vicious spirit whose grave you would not wish to disturb.

Yet that is exactly what a homeless man did in 1999. While seeking shelter he fell through the floor of the tomb. Local legend tells that when he broke into Sir George Mackenzie's mausoleum, he set the angry spirit free and so began the terrifying reign of the Mackenzie poltergeist.

Since that fateful night, there have been hundreds of reports and documented cases of people mysteriously collapsing when approaching his tomb. Many more have been pushed and pulled and received inexplicable injuries, cuts and bruises while in the vicinity of the desecrated mausoleum.

Other tourists and locals have felt cold spots, witnessed mysterious fires and scores of unexplainable animal deaths, all seemingly emanating from the poltergeist's violated resting place.

In 2004, two teenagers broke into the tomb and beheaded a corpse, using its skull as a hand-puppet. They also removed a number of unidentified items and were eventually found guilty of grave-robbing under the ancient law of 'violation of sepulchre'.

Is the poltergeist angry at being disturbed? Is *Bluidy Mackenzie* continuing his persecution of people after death, on the very same ground he tortured people in life?

Will the spirit of *Bluidy Mackenzie* ever find peace again?

Given how much Sir George Mackenzie delighted in other people's misery while alive, does it even want to?

If you take a trip to Edinburgh, you will find the doors to the mausoleum currently locked. However, you can still sneak a peek inside through the gaps.

And if you are feeling brave, you can dare the poltergeist to emerge from its tomb by reciting an old children's rhyme: "*Bluidy Mackingie, come oot if ye daur, lift the sneck and draw the bar!*"

THE GHOSTS OF CULLODEN

The Jacobite Rising came to a bloody conclusion on 16th April 1746 on the fields of Culloden. The Jacobite forces of Charles Edward Stuart were slaughtered in a brutal battle with British Government forces. It was the final blow that ended a centuries-long conflict.

The Battle of Culloden was the last pitched battle fought on British soil. The fighting itself lasted less than an hour as the Jacobite forces, hampered by the wind, rain and hail, succumbed to the government's army. When it was over, the dead and injured from both sides numbered between 1,750 to 2,400. Culloden Moor was bathed in their blood.

The Visitor Centre at Culloden Battlefield near Inverness was opened with the intention of preserving the battlefield in a similar condition to which it was fought on in 1746. You can wander across the battlefield while viewing the memorial cairn and headstones erected to commemorate the mass graves of the clans who lost brave men that day.

Local residents have reported seeing a tartan-clad spectre who wanders across the moor, whispering a single word carried on the wind – 'defeated'.

It is rumoured that birds will not sing while flying above the boggy ground. And if you dare to pay a visit on the anniversary of the battle, you might join the many people who claim to have heard gunshots, the ringing of swords and the sounds of dying men echoing across the empty moor.

THE GHOST PIPER OF CLANYARD BAY

Phantom pipers are a popular theme in Scottish urban legends and the ghost piper of Clanyard Bay combines many recurring aspects of these folktales into one legendary story.

It's said that there used to be an underground network of caves and tunnels that extended out from Clanyard Bay, located south of Stranraer.

Locals avoided the area, believing that fairies dwelled within the dark caves leading into the cliffs of the bay. However, one day a brave piper decided to explore the caves and tunnels in search of the fairies. He elected to take his faithful dog with him and play his bagpipes, so that others may know he was still alive.

Locals waited as he entered the caves, the sound of his pipes getting fainter as the hours passed. Eventually, the sound faded completely, replaced by silence.

Suddenly, the piper's dog burst from the cave with a terrifying howl. The locals gasped as they realised the dog had lost all of its hair (another common theme in these tales). The brave piper was never seen again.

Nowadays, the caves are gone, the entrance to the tunnel networks (if they truly existed) collapsed or eroded with the passage of time. What remains curious, though, are the numerous reports of people walking in the area at night who hear the sound of bagpipes being played deep underground.

THE HEADLESS DRUMMER

During the rare quiet moments at Edinburgh castle, if you listen closely, you may be able to hear the lonely rat-a-tat-tat of a ghostly headless drummer.

At dusk or dawn, or in the middle of the night, when the masses of tourists have left for the day and only a few souls remain within its walls, the drummer may emerge.

The tune he plays is thought to be a terrible one, for it's known to be a harbinger of doom for the castle, warning that great danger is coming.

The mournful beat is said to belong to the Headless Drummer Boy who haunts the castle, an apparition whose first reported sighting was in 1650.

His appearance coincided with the invasion of Scotland, and the subsequent capture of Edinburgh Castle, by Oliver Cromwell. This lead to his reputation as a bad omen for the current owners of the castle.

In less turbulent times, the Headless Drummer has not been seen for centuries, his loud warning no longer required in a more peaceful world where the castle is not under imminent attack.

However, the ethereal rat-a-tat-tat echoing around the castle walls in those quieter times suggests that he is still there, every-ready to step forth, should the need ever arise.

EDINBURGH PLAYHOUSE PHANTOM

Edinburgh Playhouse Theatre is the largest working non-sporting theatre in the United Kingdom, with an audience seating capacity of 3,059.

The old brick building housing the theatre has been used for many purposes over the years, including as a jousting ground in medieval times and as a cinema prior to becoming a theatre.

Much more mysterious and somewhat unnerving purposes include being used as a religious meeting place (a Tabernacle) and an insane asylum run by nuns.

The theatre also houses a grey phantom, who loves to let you know when he is around.

In the 1950s, reports began flooding in of people seeing old Albert, a ghostly figure dressed in grey. Eerily, the very first account of meeting old Albert was provided by the city police department.

Responding to reports of a break-in, the officers swept the building. Afterwards, one of the officers informed the theatre manager that the only person inside the building was an old gentleman wearing grey overalls, who said his name was Albert and he worked there as the doorman.

The confused manager informed the officer that the building was supposed to be empty and nobody of that description worked there. Another sweep of the building failed to find Albert again.

Since that first meeting, Albert has continued to make his presence felt within the building. Staff members have frequently reported hearing strange noises with no source, including the sound of an entire ghostly orchestra playing overnight on an empty stage.

Others have felt a hand on their shoulder, but when they turned, nobody was there. Many more have seen the shadowy figure of Albert dressed in grey, lurking in the halls, corridors and a specific room on level six that he likes to haunt. Staff members locking the building at night have seen a man entering a room, gone to inform him that they are closed, but found the room empty.

Nobody knows who Albert was in life. Some have suggested he worked at the theatre, either as a janitor or stagehand, who possibly died in a tragic accident inside the building. Others refer to the original police report, suggesting that Albert may have been the doorman to the building, who committed suicide, was murdered or died alone, leaving his spirit to wander the halls and corridors.

In 2005, during the G8 summit, the police sent sniffer dogs around the building. When the dogs reached the room where Albert is said to haunt, they stopped and refused to enter. Their handlers couldn't convince these highly trained animals to enter this one room.

Those hunting spirits are guaranteed to find some within the theatre bar, which is named Alberts, in honour of their ghostly resident. And if you linger long enough, maybe you will meet the man in grey overalls for yourself.

CHAPTER 4

CRIMES AND KILLERS

murder has always been a gruesome, yet fascinating, topic. Many films, TV shows and books attempt to delve into the minds of serial killers and other criminals.

Whether real or fictional, we can't help but be drawn to understand their motivations and methods. From cannibals to lethal assassins, and justice served to injustices never forgotten, these are the stories that stay with us.

In this chapter we explore what drives people to kill, as well as look at famous crimes, some of which remain unsolved to this day, adding to their legendary status.

LADY FINELLA THE KING KILLER

A legendary tale from the 14th century tells of Lady Finella, a noblewoman and Scottish assassin, who killed a king with a devious trick.

Lady Finella (often spelt in a variety of ways, such as Fenella, Finuella, Finnguala etc…) was the daughter of Cuncar, Mormaer of Angus, a man whose heritage was believed to be traced back to Pictish royalty.

Her story was told in John of Fordun's chronicles which documented a number of folklore stories. He states that Lady Finella had vowed revenge when her son was killed, most likely in battle, by King Kenneth II.

In the year 995, with support from either the king's men or his rivals, Lady Finella was able to create a death-trap around a statue of a boy.

Once lured into a cottage in Fettercairn, the king pulled the head of the statue towards him, which triggered a number of crossbows, killing him instantly.

Fleeing to the coast, Lady Finella was eventually caught at the top of a waterfall near St Cyrus on the east coast. Rather than allow herself to be captured, she leapt 150ft to her death.

It is generally agreed amongst historians that, regardless of the means, Kenneth II was indeed killed in Fettercairn. Today, the valley where Lady Finella took her life is named Den Finella.

THREE BLOODY STROKES

Legend tells of a bloody end to a dispute between two great warriors. In 1010, the Battle of Barry in Angus was an epic clash in which the Scots, believed to be led by King Malcolm II, emerged victorious against the invading Danish army.

During the battle, an ancestor of the Keith family was believed to have killed the fearsome Viking leader Camus.

However, shortly after the battle, another warrior claimed that it was actually he who had slain the great Camus.

In order to resolve the dispute, King Malcolm II ordered the two men to fight to the death in single combat. Keith emerged victorious from the battle and, as he lay dying, his opponent admitted that he had lied.

King Malcolm II stood over the body of the defeated warrior, reached down, and dipped three fingers into the pooling blood. He then wiped his fingers across Keith's shield and declared *Veritas Vincit*, which translates to *Truth Prevails* (sometimes recorded as *Truth Prevails* or *Truth Overcomes*).

Some accounts say that it was Camus' blood used to make the marks that day.

The three bloody strokes the king created on the shield are still worn with pride on the red and gold striped design of the Keith family coat of arms to this day, and his words became the family motto.

THE BODY OF NETTA FORNARIO

One of the most mysterious unexplained deaths to have intrigued investigators for nearly one hundred years is that of Netta Fornario. She was a resident on the island of Iona, which lies in the Inner Hebrides.

Ancient Celtic legend tells that Iona Abbey may have been where the Book of Kells was created, an illuminated manuscript containing the four Gospels of the New Testament.

It is still a place of Christian pilgrimage to this day but has been used as the site of sacred ceremonial worship long before Christianity came to the island. But for one unfortunate woman, the island seemingly appeared to harbour much darker secrets.

In November 1929, the body of 33-year-old Netta, formally named Nora Emily Fornario, was found in the centre of a field.

She was completely naked, save for a mysterious black cloak. Her body was positioned to adorn a cross carved into the earth of the field. Her feet were covered in scratches and a discarded knife lay next to her body.

Were the cross, knife and cloak evidence that a darker ritual or formal ceremony had taken place?

Why did the family she stayed with on the island report that her silver jewellery had turned black?

Scottish author, William Sharp, had indicated that fairies existed on Iona, something that was believed to be of great interest to Netta.

Occultist, Dion Fortune, suggested this may have been the reason that Netta travelled to the island. A former friend of Netta's, Dion began to distance herself from the friendship as the sheer extent of her involvement with the occult grew.

Netta was raised in London by her wealthy grandfather and had become a member of the Alpha et Omega occult society. Members of these secretive societies would learn as much as they could about ancient ways of magic, ceremonial rituals and communion with spirits, demons and other creatures not of this world. They would then practice them with wild abandon.

Upon her arrival at Iona, it's known that Netta stayed with the MacRae family. They reported that she displayed odd behaviours, including wandering around vacantly and sometimes entering trances and speaking incomprehensible sentences.

Netta told the MacRae family that she was being telepathically attacked by others on the island. Then on that fateful day in November, the family caught her hurriedly packing her belongings.

When questioned, she told them that she believed she was going to be physically attacked by some of the island's residents.

In her hurry to leave, she overlooked the fact that it was Sunday. This meant that no ferries were leaving the island until the next day.

After a long wait at the ferry port, she returned to the MacRae's home, left her belongings there and said she was going for a walk. That was the last time anybody saw her alive.

The next day a member of the MacRae family discovered that Netta was missing. Her room was neatly arranged, suggesting she had not returned from her walk.

A search ensued, but nobody could find her. It wasn't until the following day that her body was found in a hollow in the field, next to a fairy mound.

It's unknown who carved the cross into the earth, but it's believed to be part of a ritual to commune with the faerie realm, only adding to the mystery surrounding her final moments.

Given that it was November on an isolated Scottish island, one would assume that her naked body had died of exposure. However, if this was the case, then why were her feet covered in scratches, suggesting she had been running away from someone, or something?

Her death was officially recorded as heart failure from exposure. To this day, she still lies buried on the island, her secrets carried to the grave.

THE BURNING BISHOP

A Scottish bishop met a grisly end while attempting to raise taxes for the local church. Adam Melrose was the bishop of Caithness, based in Halkirk. At that time Caithness was part of the Jarldom of Orkney, which belonged to the Kingdom of Norway.

Adam had upset the locals by increasing the episcopal tax that the husbandmen of Caithness must pay. He had declared that the tax would be a span of butter from every ten cows, instead of every twenty, doubling the tax due. Unfortunately for Adam, he was about to discover why it's not a good idea to upset a Highlander.

Infuriated by what they saw as unfair demands, the husbandmen took their complaint to the Jarl, Jon Haraldsson. However, the Jarl had his own agenda and used their anger to his advantage, declaring that:

"The Devil take the bishop and his butter; you may roast him if you please!"

Taking the Jarl's advice literally, that's exactly what they did. On 11th September 1222, the husbandmen gathered outside Adam's residence in Halkirk and began to chant *"Roast him alive!"*

Some had come armed with a variety of makeshift weapons and the intent to use them. What they didn't know was that their actions were about to become folklore, and would lead to their own unexpected downfall, with far worse repercussions than a butter tax.

Swept up by the fervour of the crowd, and with the lure of lower taxes, the husbandmen's anger overcame their better judgement and, after initial discussions failed, they stormed the church.

The mob trampled to death a poor monk, Serlo, Dean of Newbattle, a close friend and advisor to Adam, who happened to be in their way.

The now terrified Adam attempted to offer the men better terms, but the time for negotiations had passed.

The husbandmen seized the ill-fated Adam, dragged him into his own kitchen, smothered him in the butter he so dearly desired and then roasted him alive.

In doing so, they had unwittingly played their part in a much larger power struggle.

Their actions allowed King Alexander II to lay claim to the mainland part of the Jarldom. Visiting Caithness in person, he hung or mutilated almost all of the husbandmen involved.

The bishop's body, retrieved from his burned down kitchen, was interred into the church of Skinnet. His death is recounted in the Old Norse short narrative (þáttr) Brenna Adams byskups.

Once Adam's successor, the renowned Gilbert de Moravia (Saint Gilbert of Dornoch), was in position, he decided to move Adam's body to the Cathedral of Dornoch.

SAWNEY BEAN

One of the more famous Scottish legends, the cannibal Sawney Bean is considered to be a reflection of how the Scots were viewed by their English neighbours centuries ago. It's also an immersive tale built into one of Scotland's most popular tourist attractions, which allows you to experience being hunted and captured by Sawney Bean and his family of cannibals.

During the 1500s, legend tells that Sawney Bean and his family inhabited the caves between Girvan and Ballantrae. For reasons unknown, the family became cannibals and would kidnap travellers who strayed too close to their territory.

Alexander 'Sawney' Bean and his forty-five member clan were supposedly responsible for over 1,000 murders over a twenty-five year period. *The Newgate Calendar* reported that Sawney Bean was born in East Lothian. His father was a hard-working man who would dig ditches and trim hedges for a living, but Sawney quickly realised that he had much darker interests than his father.

The publication goes on to describe how Sawney abandoned his family home, leaving with a 'vicious' woman and suspected witch named "*Black*" Agnes Douglas. They accumulated wealth through robbing and fed themselves by eating their victims.

Their main cave was inaccessible at high tide and over 200 yards deep, allowing them to hide for many years. The couple apparently had eight sons, six daughters, eighteen grandsons and fourteen granddaughters. Many of these grandchildren were said to be the result of incestuous unions between their sons and daughters.

The entire brood would hunt at night, pickling the remains of their victims in barrels. Locals noticed the growing number of disappearances and questioned why there were so many discarded body parts washing up on beaches but were unable to determine the cause.

Unfortunately, many innocent innkeepers were lynched by angry mobs seeking justice, as they were often the last people to see the victims alive.

The first evidence of this tale is recorded in 1734 when tensions were high between England and Scotland. This was due to the new Union with Scotland Act 1706 passed by the Parliament of England and the Union with England Act 1707 passed by the Parliament of Scotland.

These two Acts of Union put into effect the terms of the Treaty of Union and led to Scotland and England being "United into One Kingdom by the Name of Great Britain".

Scotland and England had shared a king for most of the previous century, but England wanted this formal alliance to ensure this continued. Scotland was more opposed to the treaty, claiming only an independent Scottish parliament could improve conditions for Scottish people. At the time of writing, these points are still a theme within modern political discourse.

What, then, does this have to do with Sawney Bean and his family of cannibals?

The legend goes that the family ambushed a married couple who had been visiting the nearby 'fayre', but the man was extremely skilled in combat and carried a sword and pistol. He held them off long enough that a large group of fayre-goers appeared, scaring off the attackers. The survivor's story reaches the ear of the king, who arrests the family in their gore-filled caves. Sawney Bean and his entire family are then executed.

So the king puts down the savage Scottish cannibal. According to Sandy Hobbs, an academic psychologist and folklorist (a man I can relate to), 'Sawney' was actually used by the English as a derogatory term for a Scotsman.

Therefore, with no actual evidence that the family existed, the entire legend could simply be anti-Scottish propaganda designed to reinforce scaremongering and justification at the time for 'controlling' Scotland through these Acts of Union.

Hobbs states that Sawney Bean was not mentioned in any Scottish sources until 1843, with the legend originating solely from England. By this time, it had already been accepted as a part of Scottish folklore.

Today, one of the rooms within the Edinburgh Dungeon runs the Sawney Bean experience. However, for more adventurous legend seekers, there is also a cave near Bennane Head in South Ayrshire that is actually called Sawney Bean's Cave.

THE PROVAN HALL MURDERER

Provan Hall consists of two parallel buildings built in the 15th century, making it one of the oldest buildings in Glasgow. With an enclosed courtyard, the buildings were formerly used by the bishops of Glasgow as a hunting lodge. Under private ownership, it's believed to have been frequented by King James V and Mary Queen of Scots.

There have been numerous reports of paranormal activity within the hall. Ghostly apparitions have been said to appear within the buildings and at windows, each of which come with their own myth.

In 2005, a medium conducting a paranormal investigation appeared to make contact with the most famous of the resident ghosts, a spirit known as the man with the dagger. He's also more commonly known as the Provan Hall murderer.

Legend has it that this man had been away fighting in the war for two years. When he returned home, he found his wife had a child and flew into a fit of rage, stabbing his wife to death and slitting the child's throat. All of this took place in the master bedroom, where his angry spirit is said to linger still. But he's not the only ghost at the hall.

Reston Mather was the last private owner of Provan Hall and he died there in 1934, having suffered from breathing difficulties. He's said to haunt a particular staircase dressed in black, with a bowler hat and long white beard. Those using the staircase have also reported unusual breathing difficulties.

A more famous ghostly resident said to haunt the hall is that of William Baillie, who it is rumoured had an affair with Mary Queen of Scots when she stayed there for six weeks as a guest of the Baillie family.

Her father, King James V, is also thought to haunt the hall, as a medium sensed the spirit of a man of small stature, with curly hair and a beard, matching his description.

One of the most commonly sighted ghosts within the hall, usually spied from outside the building, is that of a woman and a young boy. Nobody knows who they were in life, but they are often seen peering out from windows on the upper floor by staff, visitors and people passing the hall.

They are said to have tragically lost their lives within the upper levels of the hall and have joined the Provan Hall murderer and other spirits who frequent its rooms, stairways and corridors.

CHAPTER 5

MONSTER MYTHS

Monster legends often involve battles with great mythical beasts, usually with an accompanying story designed to teach us all a valuable life lesson.

But there are also those whispered tales of monsters lurking closer to home. Not fantastical creatures, but simple vampire-like shadows with iron teeth that parents use to make their children go to sleep at night.

This chapter explores some of these monster myths, attempting to determine fact from fiction, as we learn that sometimes the real monsters are revealed by our own human nature.

JENNY WI' THE IRON TEETH

Glasgow, 1954: times are tough for a lot of people, and south of the River Clyde lies a group of tenements known as the Gorbals, an over-populated and poverty-stricken area of the city.

According to local legend at the time, this impoverished area was the hunting ground for a creature known as the Gorbals Vampire.

One dark night in September, the police were called to Glasgow's Southern Necropolis. There they found hundreds of angry children armed with a variety of knives, stakes and other pointed weapons.

The young crowd had even brought dogs with them to hunt the 7ft tall vampire who they claimed had iron teeth and was responsible for the deaths of two local children.

However, records show that not only did their search not discover any vampire activity, but there had been no reports of any disappearance or murders of children in that area for the entire year.

So what was the true cause of this panicked community?

Popular films, comics and other media of the time were blamed for the hunt. But there must be some shred of truth in there that mustered these people into action?

The graveyard itself backed onto an ironworks, whose industrial work would sometimes turn the night sky red.

Children could play and hide in the long shadows the building cast across the necropolis. But why did the vampire have iron teeth?

Certainly, there was a comic entitled Dark Mysteries #15 which contained a story by Hy Fleishman entitled *The Vampire with the Iron Teeth.* Was this where the children had got the idea to go vampire hunting that night? Or did they find inspiration closer to home?

Local legend told of an ogre that lived in a house near Glasgow Green, which is located close to the necropolis in which the children gathered that night. This may give a clue to the real-life origins of the Gorbals Vampire.

For it's known that living in that house were two elderly women, one of whom had taken a visit to a 'dodgy dentist' and emerged with a mouth full of iron fillings exposed to the world. She became known locally as Jenny Wi' the Iron Teeth.

This nickname may have come from an 1879 poem by Alexander Anderson called *Jenny wi the airn teeth*, which was taught in some schools around that time period.

The imagination of young minds may then have combined and embellished these various influences until the children had been whipped into a vampire-hunting frenzy.

Or, perhaps, the Gorbals Vampire simply evaded capture that night, and is still out there somewhere, patiently grinding his iron teeth.

THE MONSTER OF GLAMIS

Victorian folklore speaks of a monster kept inside a secret chamber deep within Glamis Castle in Angus. However, this was not a traditional folktale beast terrorising the building. Instead, it was believed to be the deformed figure of a child that the world had been told was dead.

Thomas Lyon-Bowes was born into a future royal bloodline on 21st October 1821 and, according to official records, died shortly after birth on that same day. His parents, Thomas and Charlotte Lyon-Bowes, were the great, great grandparents of Queen Elizabeth, the Queen Mother.

A tragedy, then, or so it would seem to the outside world.

In the words of Claude Bowes-Lyon, the grandfather of the Queen Mother, who inherited the Earldom in 1865:

"If you could even guess the nature of this castle's secret, you would get down on your knees and thank God it was not yours."

Could he have been referring to the accusation that Thomas had, in fact, survived the birth and was raised within a hidden chamber? This was certainly the popular opinion.

According to legend, one of the midwives who had been present at the birth was whispering to locals that Thomas was alive, which is why there was no gravestone raised for the child.

Another gentleman who did some work at the castle had also apparently been offered a sum of money to emigrate to Australia after he had met Thomas walking the passageways close to the chapel.

Was this the same estate manager who locals say refused to return to the castle once he had learned the purpose of its secret chamber?

Unfortunately, the secret chamber was no longer a family secret, though it was still well-hidden. Across Europe and North America, newspapers spoke with curiosity about the mysterious room with an unknown purpose built deep within the Scottish castle.

They all believed it held a monster.

In 1830, Sir Walter Scott mentioned the eerie night he spent at Glamis Castle, referring directly to the secret chamber.

In 1908, *Notes and Queries* (published by Oxford University Press) discussed the monster, claiming that:

"In this chamber is confined a monster, who is the rightful heir to the title and property, but who is so unpresentable that it is necessary to keep him out of sight and out of possession."

This led to a group of guests at the castle searching for the elusive monster. Their plan involved hanging towels from the windows of every room to which they had access, so they may find which one belonged to the secret chamber.

Upon looking at their work, they discovered one window did not have a towel hanging, yet no door within the castle could be found that led to this room.

Given what we now know about genetic science, it's plausible that rumours of his monstrous form may have come from a birth defect. This theory was suggested by Jacynth Hope-Simpson in her book *Who Knows?* where she indicates that it may possibly be due to his parents being closely related, as they were first cousins once removed.

Katherine and Nerissa Bowes-Lyon, cousins of the current queen, were both born with mental disabilities and spent the majority of their lives in homes and hospitals, shunned by their family. Nerissa passed away in 1986, and Katherine in 2014, but both had been listed in *Burke's Peerage* as deceased since the 1963 edition.

However, historian Mike Dash may have discovered a darker purpose for the secret chamber. He suggests that the chamber holds the remains of a murdered family.

One night, rivals from the Ogilvy clan sought refuge at the castle. Upon entering, they were herded into the secret chamber, where they were then locked inside until they starved to death. Dash suggested that the Lyons family were keen to hide the evidence of their murderous act.

Whether monster or murder, the castle has kept its secret to this day. Why not pay it a visit for yourself and see if you can work out which of its many windows may be shedding light onto its darkest secret.

THE UNICORN WOMAN

In 1671, medical professionals were presented with the curious case of a woman who had what appeared to be a unicorn's horn growing from the centre of her forehead. The eleven inch long horn was successfully removed and donated to Edinburgh University, where it is kept today in the Anatomical Collections. Attached to the horn is a small silver medallion that reads:

"This horn was cut by Arthur Temple, Chirurgion, out of the head of Elizabeth Low, being three inches above the right ear, before thir witnesses Andrew Temple, Thomas Burne, George Smith, John Smytone and James Twedie, the 14 of May 1671. It was agrowing 7 years, her age 50 years."

The horn resembles the width and texture of a ram's horn and is curled into the shape of a question mark. However, it is her compassionate treatment and removal of the horn that is most peculiar.

At that time, many people were obsessed with looking for signs of witchcraft. A young woman with a horn protruding from her head would surely have been an easy target for the witch-hunters. You can visit the Anatomical Museum and see the legendary horn for yourself.

In modern times, others have presented with similar growths, or 'cornu cutaneum', a type of skin tumour. In 2015, an 87-year-old woman from China, Liang Xiuzhen, became famous for a 13cm long horn on her head, which had started out as nothing more than a black mole.

THE BLUE MEN OF MINCH

Legend tells of mysterious and elusive creatures with blue skin that live in the water between the Isle of Lewis and mainland Scotland.

In 1917, the creatures were described in a book called *Wonder Tales from Scottish Myth and Legend* by Donald Alexander Mackenzie.

Donald stated that:

"*They are of human size, and they have great strength. By day and by night they swim round and between the Shant Isles, and the sea there is never at rest… The Blue Men wear blue caps and grey faces which appear above the waves that they raise with their long restless arms.*"

The Blue Men were also known as Storm Kelpies and they are said to skim lightly beneath the surface of the water, always on the lookout for unwary sailors so that they may sink their boats and drown their crew.

This is why Mackenzie said they would splash with mad delight when a storm was brewing, as they knew that they would soon be able to cause mischief.

The origins of this tale are unknown. Some have suggested that they may have been Moorish slaves attempting to escape to freedom, their bodies becoming blue once the cold of the water had taken hold. This would explain the 'splashing around' used to describe their behaviour.

Or perhaps the mythical creatures were simply Picts, who would paint their bodies and cross the sea in low-lying boats, which may have looked like blue men rising from beneath the waves.

Or could their riddle have been solved by a modern-day 'blue man'? Paul Karason, also known as *Papa Smurf,* became famous due to his skin turning blue. His condition was the result of a medical condition called argyria, or silver poisoning caused by dietary supplements.

Paul drank ten ounces of colloidal silver every day, mixed in water. He believed it cured arthritis in his shoulders and his acid reflux issue.

Had the people living around the Isle of Lewis at this time took to drinking silver-laced concoctions? Maybe as part of a long-forgotten medicinal or ritual purpose? Or is there yet another explanation offered by modern science?

The Blue Fugates of Kentucky were the result of six generations of a genetic anomaly and inbreeding. The rare blood disorder they carried meant that their skin was blue, due to a lack of oxygenated blood. Both parents need to carry the rare recessive gene responsible, in order to have a blue baby.

Could this have been the case then for The Blue Men of Minch? There have certainly been other cases of blue babies being born throughout the world. Until the day the Blue Men return, this mystery will remain unsolved.

THE ZOMBIE PRIEST

St Mary's Abbey, Melrose is a partly ruined monastery located in Roxburghshire. More commonly known as Melrose Abbey, the gothic building is an ancient Scottish landmark and the burial place of Alexander II, as well as other Scottish kings and nobles. However, legend says that one of its inhabitants returned from the dead.

Hunderprest, a priest at the abbey, had gained a reputation for regularly slipping in his spiritual duties. In particular, he had a fondness for hunting with dogs and a deep passionate lust for his mistress.

In the spring of 1196, Hunderprest passed away and his corpse was buried in the graveyard at the abbey. But he did not remain buried for long.

Historian William of Newburgh was the first to tell the story of Hunderprest returning from the dead to terrorise the priests, his wails ringing out in the night as he wandered across the nearby lands.

In the book *Vampires Through the Ages: Lore & Legends of the World's Most Notorious Blood Drinkers*, author Brian Righi also tells the tale of the undead priest. He states that Hunderprest had attempted to break into the abbey, but was held back by his former priesthood brothers through the power of prayer. Righi writes:

"Forced away, the revenant roamed the countryside making terrible noises until it reached the bedchamber of its former mistress."

Seemingly drawn to the places he frequented in life, the zombie priest apparently returned to his mistress on several occasions.

Eventually, the poor woman, no longer attracted to the rotting Hunderprest, begged the friary for help. This led to a team of four monks being formed, with one purpose. To kill Hunderprest, and make sure he stayed dead this time.

One night the four brave monks gathered at the zombie priest's tomb. Three of them, succumbing to the cold, left to warm themselves at a nearby house. Righi writes:

"No sooner had they passed from view than the revenant appeared to the remaining monk and rushed upon him with a terrible noise. The monk remained firm."

The fourth monk is then thought to have struck the zombie priest with his axe, forcing the creature to return to his tomb.

When the four monks returned to the grave in the morning, they discovered that there was indeed an axe wound on Hunderprest's body, and blood was still pouring freely from the injury.

Deciding that death by fire may be the only way to set their former brother at rest, the monks cremated Hunderprest and scattered his ashes far and wide. Whether the events in this legend occurred or not, historian Stephen R Gordon believes that it serves as a cautionary tale for those who would over-indulge in earthly pleasures.

THE NINE MAIDENS OF DUNDEE

The legend goes that there was a farmer who lived on a farm called Pitempton with his nine beautiful daughters. After toiling in the fields all day, the farmer asked the eldest of his daughters to fetch some water from the nearby well. Having been gone a rather long time, the tired farmer then sent the next eldest daughter to find the first.

This continued until the farmer had sent away all his daughters, but none had returned. When he left the farm to investigate their disappearance, he discovered the dead bodies of his nine daughters discarded on the ground near the well. And there, laying in the blood of its victims, the farmer saw a huge dragon with a coiled, serpent-like body.

Afraid for his own life, the farmer ran away and alerted his neighbours, who returned to the well armed with a variety of weapons, determined to slay the dragon.

Sensing the danger it was now in, the dragon attempted to flee. However, a young man named Martin was able to catch the beast before it took flight, striking it down with his wooden club. The crowd roared 'Strike, Martin' as he defeated the huge serpent.

To recognise his heroic deed, the site where the dragon was slain was named Strike-Martin. Later, this was again renamed to Strathmartine. Travellers to the northern edge of Dundee can view Martin's Stone, which lies in a field north of Bridgefoot, which itself was formerly named Kirkton of Strathmartine. On Dundee High Street, visitors can also see a statue of the dragon.

THE STOOR WORM

In Norse mythology, Jörmungandr (meaning 'huge monster') is the Midgard (World) Serpent. According to Norse legend, Odin cast Jörmungandr into the ocean, where he grew so large that he encircled the world and grasped his own tail. Ragnarök, the Old Norse end of the world, was said to begin when he finally released his tail.

This Norse legend is thought to have been adapted by people living in the Orkney Islands, becoming the Stoor Worm (also known as Mester Stoor Worm). This sea serpent was said to have putrid breath that would contaminate crops, kill animals and harm humans.

It was believed that each Saturday, at sunrise, the Stoor Worm would wake from its slumber, open its mouth and yawn nine times. It's said that a king was advised by a sorcerer that the beast must be fed a meal of seven virgins to appease his appetite. Failing that, the king must sacrifice his own daughter, Princess Gem-de-lovely.

The king, concerned by the beast's imminent arrival and distraught by the requirement to sacrifice a daughter, offered his own daughter's hand in marriage (and the magical sword Sickersnapper, inherited from Odin) to anyone who could rid the world of the monster.

Tempted by the king's offer, Assipattle, the seventh son of a good-hearted local farmer, planned to defeat the beast himself. Known as a lazy daydreamer who would often spin tales of himself fighting imaginary foes, he was roundly ridiculed when he announced his plan.

Meanwhile, to save his daughter, the desperate king made plans to fight the Stoor Worm himself using Sickersnapper. He had his guards ready his boat at the water's edge and was due to set sail the following morning.

Undeterred by the mocking laughter of his family, Assipattle stole his father's horse during the night and set off in search of the creature. Arriving just as the great serpent opened its mouth at sunrise, the resourceful Assipattle stole some hot peat from an elderly woman's cottage and tricked the king's guard into giving him the boat meant for the king.

During one great yawn, Assipattle sailed the boat down into the creature's stomach. There he plunged the burning peat into the liver of the great beast, starting a blaze and causing the Stoor Worm to retch, which carried his boat back out of the monster's mouth to the safety of the crowded beach.

The islanders watched the Stoor Worm's death throes from the safety of a nearby hillside, out of reach of the great waves, earthquakes and plumes of black smoke emanating from the creature. As it died, its teeth fell out and became the islands of Orkney, Shetland and the Faroes. Its body became Iceland and its tongue created the Baltic Sea.

The king kept his word and awarded Assipattle both the magic sword and Princess Gem-de-lovely's hand in marriage. It's said that the celebrations lasted for nine weeks and they lived happily ever after. A lesson, then, to never give up on your daydreams.

THE LOCH NESS MONSTER

No book of urban legends would be complete without including one of Scotland's most famous and enduring mysteries.

The Loch Ness Monster (known fondly as *Nessie*) is believed to be a dinosaur-like creature which inhabits Loch Ness. Often reported to have a long neck and humps, the first recorded sighting of Nessie was nearly 1,500 years ago when an unfortunate farmer was apparently eaten by a large beast erupting from Loch Ness.

In 1934, the legend gained momentum when a London doctor produced a photograph that appeared to show Nessie protruding from the water.

There have been many more sightings over the years, despite the British Broadcasting Corporation (BBC) completing an extensive search of the loch in 2003. Using 600 sonar beams and satellite tracking, the BBC appeared to have concluded that Nessie was a myth.

Some of these sightings have been shown to be hoaxes.

But many others provide compelling arguments which ensure, if nothing else, that the legend of Nessie isn't going away any time soon.

You can read a more detailed account of the hunt for The Loch Ness Monster, and a host of other fascinating creatures from Scottish folklore, in my bestselling book: *Scottish Legends: 55 Mythical Monsters.*

THE BONELESS

Legend tells that many years ago a strange blob-like creature washed up on the shores of the Shetland Islands, bringing with it much malevolence and misfortune. The Boneless (also known by locals as the Frittening) was a creature straight out of Shetland folklore that terrified the locals. Accounts recall how the creature exuded a disgusting smell that sickened those who smelled it and unleashed disease upon the islands.

The large jelly-fish like blob is described as being pale, with a surface that is constantly shifting. It's thought to bring bad luck for all who encounter it, and if you stare at its surface for too long you lose your mind, making detailed accounts of its appearance difficult to capture.

Explanations for the 'blob' range from being an alien, a giant jellyfish or an as yet unidentified sea creature, perhaps from prehistoric times. It arrives and departs with the tides, bringing misfortune to any who discover it while it is washed up on the shore.

Believed to be a generally mindless creature, but with hunting instincts, stories have emerged of the Boneless leaving the shore when the veil between our world and the spirit world is at its thinnest. At these times the creature travels inland, attacking homes and people. During one of these incidents, the Boneless grabbed a young boy during the night and wrapped itself around him as it dragged him back towards the water. Fortunately, the boy kept his wits about him and recited The Lord's Prayer, causing the creature to release him and retreat back to the sea.

CHAPTER 6

CURIOUS AND UNEXPLAINED

Unexplained mysteries and curious oddities are littered throughout Scottish history, waiting to be discovered by inquisitive minds.

The story of a proud witch is told alongside that of a seer with frighteningly accurate prophecies. There are mysterious disappearances, strange weather, suicide ghosts and a legendary Scottish figure.

This chapter explores myths surrounding the origins of Scottish symbols, such as the saltire and thistle. It also contains personal stories and experiences that have never been published before.

THE SALTIRE

The Saltire. the national flag of Scotland, consists of a white cross laid diagonally across a blue field and is a symbol of great national pride.

Legend says that in 60 AD, when Saint Andrew, the patron saint of Scotland and one of the Apostles, was about to be crucified, he refused to be placed upon a traditional T-shaped cross.

His reasoning for this was that he considered himself unworthy to be crucified on a cross similar to that of Jesus Christ, and so was nailed to an X-shaped cross instead, also known as a saltire.

This became his symbol and is why the Scottish flag is often referred to as St. Andrew's cross.

But how did Scotland come to adopt the saltire?

Another legend says that in 832 AD, a great battle was about to take place in Lothian between a Pictish army and a Northumbrian army. Completely surrounded by their enemies on all sides, the Picts prayed for help.

The night before the battle, Saint Andrew appeared before the Pictish army and assured them of victory. The next day, as the confrontation was about to take place, both sides looked up to see a great white saltire spread across the sky. The Northumbrian army, alarmed by this clear sign of support for their enemies, decided to retreat, and thus the Picts were victorious.

THE BRAHAN SEER

Kenneth the Sallow (also known as Coinneach Odhar or Dark Kenneth) was a man gifted with an ability known as *The Second Sight* or *Two Sights*.

Day or night, Kenneth could suddenly become struck with visions of the future, which often resulted in him predicting future events. The accuracy of his prophecies earned him the nickname The Brahan Seer.

Born Kenneth Mackenzie in the 17th century, he lived beside Loch Ussie, near Dingwall. He spent his days quietly working away as a labourer on the Brahan estate, which at the time was the seat of the Seaforth chieftains.

However, it quickly became known that Kenneth was gifted with the ability to view two worlds at once, this one and a future one.

While this ability is often deliberately sought after by those dabbling in witchcraft, it's actually viewed as a curse in Scotland, due to the bearer having no control over when and where this Second Sight will take hold.

Legend suggests that the origins of his affliction are due to an encounter his mother had one night with the ghost of a Danish princess.

Blocking the poor spirit's way to the graveyard, his mother demanded that the ghost pay a tribute in order to return to her tomb. Her request was that her son would be gifted with *The Second Sight*.

Elsewhere, later that day, Kenneth was out walking when he happened upon a small stone with a hole bored through the middle. When he looked through the hole, his gift was bestowed and he had his first vision.

Kenneth found that, in addition to the visions that afflicted him against his will, he could also use the small stone he found to gain glimpses of the future.

Known as an Adder Stone, these naturally occurring objects were believed the world over to be used in witchcraft, often being referred to as hag stones, druid stones or serpent's eggs.

The reason Kenneth's story has survived through the ages is the accuracy with which he apparently predicted certain future events.

On a particular Scottish moor, he stated:

"Oh! Drumossie, thy bleak moor shall, ere many generations have passed away, be stained with the best blood of the Highlands. Glad am I that I will not see the day, for it will be a fearful period; heads will be lopped off by the score, and no mercy shall be shown or quarter given on either side."

This moor would become the site of the Battle of Culloden.

One very specific prediction he made was that Scotland would one day have its own Parliament, but not before *men could walk dry shod from England to France.*

Shortly after the Channel Tunnel opened, so too did the new Scottish Parliament.

One day, while on a walk with a friend, the seer pointed to a field and foretold that "*A village with four churches will get another spire and a ship will come from the sky and moor at it.*"

In 1932 an airship was forced to make an emergency landing at a village now built on that field. It was tied to the spire of the newly-built church.

Kenneth also stated that "*A black rain will bring riches to Aberdeen.*" Predicting the discovery of oil in the North Sea.

He also predicted the laying of modern utility pipes, such as gas and water, when he said that *streams of fire and water would run beneath the streets of Inverness and into every house.*

Two hundred years prior to their arrival, he predicted that railways would be built throughout the Highlands, describing "*Great black brideless horses, belching fire and steam, drawing lines of carriages through the glens.*"

Another vision to come true was when Kenneth stated that "*The sheep shall eat the men.*"

Many believe he had foreseen the Highland Clearances, a period of unrest where landowners forcibly removed families from their homes and their farms became grazing land for sheep.

However, one fateful night, The Brahan Seer made a final honest prediction, that resulted in his death. His services were called upon by Isabella, the wife of the Earl of Seaforth, who wished to hear news of her husband, who was in Paris at the time.

Kenneth received his vision, but would only tell Isabella that her husband was in good health. This angered her and she demanded to be given a full and honest account of what the vision had shown him, or he would be put to death.

Kenneth sombrely foretold that, not only was the Earl with another woman in Paris but that the Seaforth line would come to an end when their final heir was born deaf and dumb. Isabella, whether attempting to reverse the vision or simply enraged, had her guards murder Kenneth by plunging his head into a barrel of boiling tar.

His death, though, did not stop his final prediction from coming true. In 1783, Francis Humberston Mackenzie became 1st Baron Seaforth, the last male heir of the Earls of Seaforth. A politician, soldier and botanist, Francis was also the Chief of Highland Clan Mackenzie, from which he raised the 78th (Highlanders) Regiment of Foot.

Francis had achieved much in life, considering that at age twelve he had contracted scarlet fever, which had caused him to become completely deaf and stolen almost all of his ability to speak. All four of his legitimate sons died, bringing to an end his family line, as predicted by The Brahan Seer.

WICK NORTH PRIMARY SCHOOL

The urban legends around this primary school are terrifying for two reasons. Firstly, because it was my own primary school. Secondly, because it was here that I witnessed my first unexplainable encounter that still haunts me to this day.

I would say that the majority of schools have some version of an urban legend attached to them. The ones where I grew up seemed to each have their own Grey Lady that haunted the corridors and – like a mature *Moaning Myrtle* from *Harry Potter* – lingered around the school toilets, ready to attack any young Muggles who dared to pee during school hours.

However, in an 80s-inspired twist, the boys' toilets in the North Primary School in Wick were apparently frequented by Gremlins. No doubt some Highland child had received a wonderful new pet from China, that came with very specific instructions.

Unfortunately, the little furry Mogwai had obviously escaped and sneaked into my primary school. There, it had unwittingly jumped out on a trembling child mid-flow, gotten wet, and was now bringing its mini reign of terror to bathroom trips. Fortunately, it was not a Gremlin that I witnessed that day. Though the reality is a little more frightening.

It was a warm evening and I was playing football on the ground in front of the school. From here you could see the windows into every classroom.

It was nearly time for me to go home when I glanced up at one of the windows and saw what I thought was my old primary 5 teacher looking down at us playing football.

She had long hair that hung past her shoulders and a white dress. I assumed the greyness of her figure was caused by the setting sun reflecting off the glass. I waved to her, but she didn't wave back. She just kept on staring down at us.

One of my friends asked what I was waving at, but when I went to point to the figure, she was gone.

This is when a cold chill went through me.

I explained to my friends what I had seen and that the teacher must be working late. However, when we checked the car park it was empty. We cautiously tried all the outer doors to the school.

They were all locked.

I was glad that I moved up to the high school not long after this encounter!

I told my friend, Ami MacDonald, about this story and she said that the South Primary School in Wick also had its own Grey Lady that haunted the girl's toilets.

"I think it was a ghost called the Grey Lady and she haunted the bogs! I used to run in and out, nearly tripping myself, it was brutal! But it was okay if other kids were in there. What I thought she was going to do to me I will never know."

Another well-known story amongst our group is that of our friend, Gary Robertson, who once ran around the school taunting the Grey Lady to appear.

Partway through one of his laps, his chanting resulted in roof tiles falling and nearly hitting him. Was it merely a coincidence? Maybe so, but it's one that is still remembered and talked about to this day.

It wasn't just Grey Ladies and Gremlins running loose around this school though. There was also 'the boy at the desk'.

A particular patch of the exterior wall was known to display the shadowy silhouette of a boy sitting at a school desk. Locals state that this shadow only appeared after a young boy was tragically killed in a road accident outside the school.

I have clear memories of my young mind analysing the shape and being caught up in the fervour of our group, likely high on tuck shop sugar, insisting that it was most definitely an apparition.

The shadow was more prominent when it rained and the school janitor insisted that it was simply a damp patch that just happened to be in a familiar shape.

Regardless, all of these spirits will now find themselves homeless after the school building was sadly demolished. But they will live on in the memories of those of us who learned at an early age to hold our pee in for eight hours straight.

FAMILY VISITORS

One of the most commonly shared paranormal experiences that people have is seeing the ghost of a loved one. These deeply personal visitations can be both a comfort and completely terrifying. This is a story of three families and three ghostly visitors.

I am a self-proclaimed sceptic, but it's known that our Mullins family surname descends from our mystical Celtic origins. The majority of my family are Scottish, but our Irish ancestors had actually travelled over from Cork.

The women in our family tree were famous clairvoyants, known for their ability to accurately predict future events. As a young adult, you have no idea how difficult it is to lie to somebody with a hint of the mystic in their blood - 'my ESP is telling me you were not at the library, which closed four hours ago, but were actually drinking up the riverside' – I shrug, swaying slightly and cursing my ancestors as I prepare to receive a broomstick over my head.

Despite my scepticism and the science of the modern world, even I have to admit that I have witnessed things that I can't explain. Visits from my deceased grandmother is one of them.

During her life, my grandma believed that she had a spirit guide with whom she could converse. When this guide spoke of me, he would refer to me as '*the writer*', long before I had ever sat down and typed up my first story as an adult.

I used to think this was something she said to try and motivate me to write, as if it would become a self-fulfilling prophecy from which my writer credentials would manifest.

But now, after my grandma has passed and my books have achieved bestseller status, I do wonder whether the reason this spirit was a 'guide' is because he could see the future?

During the night, for about a week, I would get sudden whiffs of my grandma's perfume in my bedroom. Then one night, something unexplainable occurred.

My young daughter would often climb out of her bed and wander through to us in a half-asleep state, where she would stand beside the bed until my wife reached out and guided her in the dark to climb into bed. The scraping of the door on the carpet would wake us both up, she would grab her, then we would all go back to sleep.

However, one night the door scraped open, we woke up and my wife reached out to guide my daughter. Except all she could feel was air. She whispered my daughter's name. The door then closed.

Thinking that our daughter was so sleepy she had become confused, my wife got out of bed to make sure she didn't bump into anything while wandering around in the dark. What she discovered was that our daughter was in her own bed, fast asleep. There was no way she could have got back there in the short time that had passed. It was then that we got the strongest whiff of my grandma's perfume in the air.

Suffice to say the bedroom was so lit up for the rest of the night that it could probably have been seen from space.

I told this story to my friend Donald Mackay, fully expecting to be ridiculed for my 'fanciful' imaginings. Instead, he told me his own tale of a family visitor from beyond the grave.

Donald is a friend I have known since childhood. Even back then he was a stoically independent Highlander in both his words and actions.

Now he's a strong and dependable family man with a management career who would not usually have time for such trivial nonsense as ghosts. So if this man tells me that he seen a ghost, I would bet my life that is exactly what happened.

In 2006, Donald's mother unfortunately passed away from a brain tumour four days after his birthday. From that moment on, in the same week of October every year, the spirit of his mother has visited him.

I will let Donald tell the tale in his own words:

"Once we were in Turkey and she was standing at the end of my bed. She was saying something, but I don't know what. If I'm honest, I was terrified and screaming like a banshee. I don't believe in any of that stuff, but every October I see my mum either in the street or in my house. I class myself as a pretty strong person, but every October, for a week or so, I'm a broken man."

I understand the pain he feels of losing a parent, as my own father committed suicide in 2011. Lacking the clairvoyant abilities of my ancestors, I can only be there for my friend whenever he needs support. And try to live up to a spirit guide's long-held classification of me as '*the writer*'.

Another close friend, Frances Hamilton, read an early version of this story and told me her own unusual tale. Early one Sunday morning, Frances woke from a deep sleep, gripped with an overwhelming sense of dread.

Finding the house quiet and calm, she checked her phone to see if it had woken her up, but there were no notifications. There was nobody at the door and her son was still asleep.

She eventually assumed that she had been in the middle of a nightmare that she now couldn't remember. She dismissed the feeling and lay back down in bed.

That was when her phone rang.

It was her mother calling to tell her to come to the hospital, as her granny was there. It was only when Frances arrived at the hospital that she learned her granny had actually passed away.

And a cold chill ran through her as she realised the time of death matched the precise time she remembered seeing on her phone when she had awoken with the mysterious sense of dread.

IT'S RAINING FISH

Scotland's weather can be, at times, a little unpredictable. On rare occasions, this seems to include the ability to rain fish. On 21st April 1828, Major Forbes Mackenzie awoke to discover that one of his fields was covered in small herring, about three to four inches long.

This surprised him, as his farm in Strathpeffer was over three miles away from the sea, yet the fish were whole and healthy as if they had just been freshly caught.

Two years later, in March 1830, residents on the Isle of Islay in the Inner Hebrides also discovered their fields covered in fish, again small herring. Their appearance had followed a day of heavy rainstorms and some of the fish were still alive.

Another two years later, in June 1832, yet more small herring rained down on Castlehill in Argyllshire, which is four miles from the nearest sea.

So how did the fish get from the sea to the sky, travel inland, and then rain down on unsuspecting villagers? Modern science may have discovered the reasoning behind these urban legends.

Small tornadoes are blamed for the phenomenon. While over the sea, they form waterspouts that suck up small, light fish. The winds keep them trapped in this funnel until they run out of steam further inland when they then dump the fish onto the ground. Of course, this is theoretical, as it's difficult to witness it in action.

ROBERT THE BRUCE AND THE SPIDER

Robert the Bruce is famous for the role he played in the wars of Scottish independence. His story has been told many times in books, film and other creative outlets. Perhaps most famous of all is the encounter he had with a spider.

In 1274, Robert the Bruce was born at Lochmaben Castle. He went on to serve as Knight and Overlord of Annandale and in 1306 was crowned King of Scotland.

At the time, he used his power to try and free Scotland from the rule of its English enemy. Unfortunately for him, his forces were defeated in battle by the Earl of Pembroke at Methven, forcing him into hiding.

It's said that he spent three months living in a cave somewhere in the Western Isles, struggling with grief and uncertainty as he contemplated his next move.

However, while he was living in the cave, he observed a spider building a web at the cave entrance. The stormy Scottish weather ruined the spider's work on many occasions, but the tiny creature persevered and eventually completed its web.

Inspired by the spider's determination, Robert the Bruce found hope again and decided to carry on his fight. He is attributed with coining a popular phrase when he told his men *'If at first you don't succeed, try, try and try again.'*

QUEEN OF THE WITCHES

In keeping with the times, Scotland had a dark period of history where the populace was so concerned with witchcraft that they would accuse a great number of women of black magic and foul deeds. Throughout the 16th and 17th centuries, many innocent women were tortured and burned at the stake, in an attempt to prise confessions from them of their evil ways. However, what if one of them wasn't innocent?

Isobel Gowdie was the beautiful, crimson-haired wife of a farmer. She lived an unremarkable life in the Highland village of Auldearn, right up to the moment when she was accused of witchcraft.

It's unknown what occult behaviour or random minor transgression she committed in order to be accused of being in league with the Devil. She may not have even done anything at all, as these types of accusations were often falsehood born out of revenge, jealousy, mischief or boredom.

Unlike others though, Isobel did not deny the claims. Instead, she went into great detail about how she and her coven were given their powers from the Queen of the Faeries. She said they could fly on brooms, would often transform into animals and could cast spells on people using voodoo-like dolls.

She confessed all this without the need for torture. No record of her execution exists. She disappeared without a trace. Like magic.

THE FLANNAN ISLES LIGHTHOUSE

The Flannan Isles are an isolated group of uninhabited islands in the far north west of Scotland. Also known as the Seven Hunters, the largest of these rocky islands is called Eilean Mor, upon which sits the Flannan Isles Lighthouse.

In 1900, the lighthouse was at the centre of one of the most baffling mysteries. The three men who were charged with manning the lighthouse disappeared without a trace.

When their replacements arrived, they found the lighthouse in perfect condition, with everything in its place. It's as if the men had simply blinked out of existence. James Ducat, Thomas Marshall and Donald MacArthur were never heard from again.

They had arrived at the lighthouse in good spirits, ready to begin their two-week-long shift. On arrival, they were accompanied by Robert Muirhead, the Superintendent of Lighthouses, who carried out basic checks with the three men.

Finding everything as it should be, Robert discussed with James Ducat the issue of a strange mist that sometimes surrounded the island, making their job difficult.

The mist carried an extra danger because the men would be unable to signal for help, should they get in trouble. The lighthouse was monitored via telescope from the mainland, but when the mist rolled in, the island became hidden from view.

The logs show that the lighthouse was monitored on the 7th and 12th of December via telescope. On 15th December a passing ship noted that the lighthouse beacon was not lit, as it should have been.

The thick mist and bad weather meant that the men's replacements weren't able to reach the island until 21st December, many days after their shift should have ended.

When their replacements finally did arrive at the island, they were expecting to see a raised flag to signify that the lighthouse keepers had spotted the approaching ship and were about to deploy a rowboat. But no flag was present.

The three men also didn't respond to attempts to contact them via siren. The lighthouse remained dark and silent.

Eventually the ship was forced to launch its own landing craft, containing two men. Upon reaching the island, one of those men, Joseph Moore, raced up to the lighthouse in search of the missing men.

He found the entrance locked but fortunately had a key. Upon entering the lighthouse he found that there was no sign of life at all. There was no fire burning in the grate and the cold ash suggested it had not seen one in a while.

Peculiarly, a clock on the wall had stopped and there was an uneaten meal laid out on the table, as if somebody had set it there, but vanished before they could take the first bite.

Whatever fate had befallen the men, it had apparently happened very suddenly.

Unable to discover any clues at all of the men's whereabouts, Joseph Moore decided to remain with the three replacements on the island.

During this time they inspected the log records of the three missing men.

According to the logs, on 14th December a huge storm swept over the island. The very last entry made in the log was dated from the afternoon of 15th December. A brief entry, it simply stated:

'Storm ended, sea calm. God is over all.'

Upon examining the evidence, Superintendent Muirhead concluded that the three men must have been on the outside of the lighthouse when a large wave suddenly swept them out to sea.

While the wave theory is generally accepted as being the most likely fate of the three men, it actually leaves us with a single unanswered question.

If the men were suddenly swept out to sea by a large wave during the storm, then why was the last entry in the log added after the storm had passed, literally stating that the storm had ended and the sea was calm? The bodies of the men have never been found, so the answer to this question, like so many others, remains a mystery.

DALMARNOCK BRIDGE SUICIDE GHOST

Dalmarnock Bridge is a 200-year-old road bridge over the River Clyde in Glasgow, thought to be haunted by the ghost of a man who committed suicide there.

Furthest east of all the Glasgow bridges, it originally began life as a timber toll bridge for traffic travelling between Dalmarnock and Rutherglen. Having been replaced and upgraded over the years, the current bridge still contains the original cast iron gothic arcading parapets and ornamental outer beam fascia panels from 1891.

Many people have reported seeing a man looking forlornly down into the water, seemingly contemplating whether to jump or not. Afraid that they might be about to witness a suicide, they have approached the man, only for him to then leap into the air and disappear, never reaching the river below.

The apparition is said to look exactly like a living person, as real and solid as any other man you might meet on the bridge. Specifically, he's described as being a man around thirty years old, with short hair and black trousers protruding from the bottom of a 1930s style three quarter length coat.

First spotted in the 1970s, nobody has been able to identify who the ghost was in life, or the reason for his suicide. It may take a dedicated team of paranormal investigators willing to camp out on the bridge for an extended period of time to discover why this poor spirit keeps on reliving his death over and over again.

CHARGE OF THE TEMPLAR KNIGHTS

An enduring legend surrounding Robert the Bruce is that he won a famous battle thanks to the aid of a small band of Templar Knights. In 1314, Robert the Bruce was battling against the English, led by King Edward II, and took to the field with his army at the Battle of Bannockburn.

History does not record precisely how Robert the Bruce emerged victorious from this battle, but legend states that the Knights Templar joined the battle halfway through and were pivotal in routing the enemy forces.

The details of the huge mysterious figures on horseback vary with each account of that day, but all emphasise the important role they played in claiming victory for the Scottish leader.

Historical accounts of the battle were not recorded until long after the battle took place and there may be an alternative reason behind the origins of the tale.

Instead of being an inspiring story about a crushing victory, Robert's enemies may have in fact fabricated the story to suggest that he was an inept military leader, unable to win a battle without outside support.

There is evidence to suggest that a number of Templar Knights knew that they were about to be arrested, their order having been officially disbanded seven years prior to the battle, so they escaped to Scotland.

Perhaps, then, there is some truth to the story after all.

THE THISTLE

The thistle is one of the most recognisable Scottish symbols. But how did Scotland come to adopt this prickly and beautifully rugged flowering plant as a national emblem?

It was during the reign of Alexander III (1249-1286) that the thistle came to prominence. Legend states that King Haakon of Norway sent an army to Scotland with the intent to conquer the nation and claim it as his own. Under the cover of darkness, his army landed on the coast of Largs and removed their footwear so they could sneak up on the slumbering Scottish Clansmen and stealthily kill them in their sleep.

However, the Scots were protected by the land itself, as one of Haakon's soldiers stumbled upon a thistle in the dark. His cry of pain alerted the Clansmen, who quickly defeated the invading forces.

With so many species, nobody knows the precise type of thistle that saved the day. And with no historical evidence, nobody knows if this story is true, or merely a legend. Accepted as a symbol of Scottish resilience, silver coins were issued in 1470 featuring a thistle. In the early 16th century, the thistle was also incorporated into the Royal Arms of Scotland.

Knights of the Order of the Thistle, the highest honour in Scotland, wear badges with a thistle upon it, containing the motto '*Nemo me impune lacessit*' (No-one harms me with impunity).

THE GLASGOW COAT OF ARMS

Glasgow's Coat of Arms contains not one, but four separate legends that make up its respective symbols and emblems. All of these myths refer to the life of Glasgow's patron saint, Kentigern (also known as Mungo).

The four myths contained within the coat of arms are the tree that never grew, the bird that never flew, the fish that never swam and the bell that never rang.

The tree that never grew, now represented by a strong oak tree, was once merely the humble branch of a hazel tree. Saint Mungo was placed in charge of a holy fire at St Serf's Monastery but unfortunately fell asleep. A group of mischievous boys, jealous of St Mungo's position with St Serf, decided to extinguish the fire. Upon waking, St Mungo gathered some frozen branches from a nearby hazel tree and proceeded to pray over them. The branches burst into flame and his legendary status was sealed.

The bird that never flew refers to the wild robin tamed by St Serf, which unfortunately met an accidental end. Similar to the fire, St Mungo was held responsible for this failure but was once again able to rescue the situation through the power of prayer, restoring the robin to life.

The fish that never swam is represented on the coat of arms with a ring in its mouth. Legend has it that the King of Strathclyde gave his wife the ring as a gift, but she passed it on to a knight, who then lost it in the river (other versions say the King stole it back while the knight slept).

The king then requested that his wife show him the ring he had given her, or be put to death for disloyalty. The knight confessed to St Mungo that he had lost the ring, so a monk was sent to catch a fish from the river. When St Mungo cut the fish open, the ring was inside and was hastily returned to the Queen. Another legendary miracle then, which inspired the Bishop of Glasgow to include its symbolism within his own seal and eventually made its way onto the Glasgow Coat of Arms.

The bell that never rang refers to the belief that St Mungo still watches over the city and helps it prosper. In 1450, John Stewart, the first Lord Provost of Glasgow, designated a sum of money in his will for the purpose of creating 'St Mungo's Bell', so that the citizens of Glasgow could pray for his soul every time they heard the bell toll.

Historical records show that the bell was still in use in 1578, as an entry in the City Treasurer's accounts lists two shillings 'for one tong to St Mungowis Bell'.

St Mungo is credited with a sermon that contained the words 'Lord, let Glasgow flourish by the preaching of the word'. The abbreviated 'Let Glasgow Flourish' was thus adopted as the city's motto and included on the coat of arms.

These four legends combine to make the Glasgow Coat of Arms. As a final touch, St Mungo also appears on the coat of arms, high above the tree, the bird, the fish and the bell, with his hand raised, blessing the city he loved.

AUTHOR'S NOTES

I first started believing in ghosts when I took a genuine picture of one. My family's yacht had set sail one clear summer morning from Gosport, on the south coast of England, on a short trip over to the Channel Islands. One of our aims was to visit the German Underground Hospital on Guernsey.

Built by the hands of those forced to work for the occupying German forces, the underground hospital acted as a forward base. With over 75,000 square feet of hidden tunnels, it's the largest WW2 structure on the Channel Islands.

During the war, the cries of up to 800 injured and dying patients would echo around the rooms and tunnels of this underground hospital. Little wonder then that such a place may still contain the restless spirits of those who died there. One of which was seemingly captured by myself on my camera.

We were deep within the hospital, which is open to the public, and I was taking lots of pictures of the empty rooms and tunnels. We were the only group down there and we didn't feel any mysterious presence at all, it was all quite normal.

Until we got home.

When we uploaded the pictures to a computer we noticed that a single image contained a mysterious figure. It showed one of the tunnels apparently filled with a grey mist. Within this eerie fog was the dark shape of a tall man, his head, body, eye sockets and slightly open mouth clearly visible.

And he was walking straight towards us.

You can see the image for yourself in the book launch blog post for this book, over on my website at www.aaronmullins.com.

I posted the picture on a blog forum for a local paranormal investigation team. Once they discovered I was a psychologist, I was invited to join them on one of their overnight ghost hunts.

This is how I came to be sitting in St Mary's Guildhall in Coventry at 11pm, holding hands with strangers as we 'grounded' ourselves, before setting out in search of spirits.

There was a full complement of ghost hunting equipment, cameras, sensors, temperature gauges and other gadgets.

We also had scrying mirrors, crystals and a whole host of other ways to contact the dead. At one point I was asked to wait by myself in a pitch-black room, while everybody else begged the spirits to touch me, or move the furniture that I couldn't see...

I waited patiently, quite convinced that I was about to end up in an unsolved mystery on a Netflix documentary. But despite the desperate and somewhat gleeful pleas of my fellow ghost hunters, no spirits reached out to me.

Many strange things happened that night, but none that I would label as a genuine paranormal experience. And so I remain sceptical, but open to new evidence, should it ever present itself.

Until then, I leave you with this book and its stories. I have always found Scotland's myths, legends and folk tales to be mystical, magical, bloody, thought-provoking and insightful by turn. They help us to remember our past and make sense of our often weird and wild present.

They are us, and we are each our own story.
Make yours a good one.

Aaron Mullins

ABOUT THE AUTHOR

Aaron Mullins

Dr Aaron Mullins is an award-winning, internationally published psychologist. He's also an Amazon bestselling author and is known for exploring powerful psychological experiences in his books.

Aaron has a wealth of experience in the publishing industry, with expertise in supporting fellow authors achieve their writing goals. He started Birdtree Books Publishing where he worked as Editor-in-Chief. He also partnered with World Reader Charity, getting ebooks into Africa and sponsoring English lessons in an under-tree school in India.

Aaron taught Academic Writing at Coventry University and has achieved great success with his bestselling short story anthologies. Aaron's book How to Write Fiction: A Creative Writing Guide for Authors has become a staple reference book for writers and those interested in a publishing career.

Aaron's website, www.aaronmullins.com contains free resources to support authors with inspiration and practical help, with many writing, publishing and marketing guides.

Originally from the Scottish Highlands, Aaron spent many years south of the border but now lives by the beach on the west coast of Scotland, where he devotes most of his non-writing time to charity work, raising his daughter and travelling to beautiful places.

AVAILABLE FROM AMAZON

Mullins Collection of Best New Fiction

Explore worlds populated with strange creatures. Ghouls that feed in the darkness of the London underground in *The Orphaned City* and the strange patient who stalks the halls of a mental asylum in *Inferiority Complex*. Discover worlds where humans are the most curious of all, the charming smile of the mysterious Jack in *Knowing Jack* and the devious mind of Red in *The Path I Set Upon*.

Perhaps the next story will spark into life a new idea, the kind that Jake develops from an overheard conversation in *Dreamworld*. Or question our very existence, like the revelations of Professor Westerham in *Reflection*. It might even lead to a dangerous hunt for untold riches, which Ryan experiences in *The Hassam Legacy*.

You may discover a love for stories you wouldn't have considered before. Fiction does that to you. It draws you into its welcoming embrace. Sometimes the welcome is warm, like the strength of Helen after dealing with death in *Coming of Age*. Other times you feel an icy chill as the story grips you, like the terror that claws at Meg when she hears her parrot speak in *Scared to Death*.

Nine different worlds are waiting to be explored. Each hides a secret, a twist that awaits discovery by an adventurous reader. Welcome to our worlds.

AVAILABLE FROM AMAZON

Mullins Collection of Best New Horror

Horror. The stories that keep you awake at night. The tales that have you checking underneath the bed... or wondering whether that really is just a shadow in the corner.

In this collection, you will find early stories from four horror writers, all guaranteed to instil a feeling of dread deep within your bones as your shaking fingers struggle to turn the page.

A dark secret is revealed in *My Natalie*, a tale of vengeful love. A home with a hidden past threatens to destroy a young family in *The House.*

The restless spirit of a young girl has to deliver an important message in *Phantom Memory.* Finally, thrill-seeking Melanie gets more than she bargained for, as she explores the mysterious festival in *The Secrets of Hidden Places.*

The horror awaits…

AVAILABLE FROM AMAZON

Mysteries and Misadventures:
Tales from the Highlands

Ten tales set in the Highlands of Scotland.
True childhood secrets revealed in the Story Behind the
Stories.

In *The Road Trip,* a couple make a surprise stop at a guesthouse with a deadly history, looking for its next victims. In *Secrets of the River,* an unopened box is dragged from the river. A hastily scrawled message from the past, stolen by a young woman who is now being hunted. With time running out, can she survive its secrets?

In *Equal To and Greater Than,* James has a 1 in 54 condition. Attacked and humiliated, he must harness the power of his gifts and become the hero he needs to be. In *The Gala Queen,* it's Halloween night. A prank goes wrong. A young girl dies and the boy responsible has got away with it. Until the annual town gala, when the gala queen comes seeking vengeance.

In *Revenge of the Green Man,* Charlie plots to get his stolen CD back, dragging his friend into ever-crazier schemes. In *The House on Lovers' Lane,* a boy is missing and two girls lie to their parents so they can spend the night drinking in a field. But when a dare goes wrong they soon discover the danger they are in.

In *Call of the Nuckelavee,* a woman stalks the sandy dunes, following the voice of her drowned father. In the turbulent sea, she comes face to face with a creature that has haunted her nightmares. In *Black Dog in the Devil's Bothy*, a troubled woman hikes through a storm. She strays from the mountain path and loses her way in the forest. Taking shelter in a bothy, she discovers her fears have followed her to the darkest of places.

In *Last Train South*, a woman boards a train with a heavy suitcase. Evidence she must dispose of, with the help of her friends. In *Stolen Peace*, a nuclear biologist just wants to spend his final days camping in the woods and reading his book. Unfortunately, trained killers want him to return the item he stole.

AVAILABLE FROM AMAZON

Scottish Legends: 55 Mythical Monsters

A MAMMOTH collection of Scottish Legendary Creatures and Mythical Monsters. From Amazon bestselling author Aaron Mullins comes the ultimate guide to 55 fantastical creatures of Scottish folklore.

Discover the origins of each supernatural creature, from a land filled with werewolves, sea monsters and fiendish ghouls. Hear true accounts from people who have come face to face with these fearsome beasts and lived to tell their tale.

Stories of legendary creatures have always captured the imagination. The mythical unicorn is the national animal of Scotland and many travellers have gathered around campfires across Scottish hillsides to hear fascinating stories of mysterious blue men, sorcerous shapeshifters and ferocious sea serpents.

How can you tell if your child has become a changeling? Which female vampire hides her hooves from human eyes? Where can you capture a mermaid who will grant you three wishes?

Discover the answers to these questions and many more within this book.

AVAILABLE FROM AMAZON

Scottish Killers: 25 True Crime Stories

25 True Crime Stories of Murder and Malice

A fascinating collection of Scotland's most deadly serial killers and notorious murderers.

A chilling anthology of the true crime stories that shocked the world.

The details of each case are revealed.
The motives of each killer are explored.

Each murder is examined in a new light, stripped of the sensationalism of newspapers, and with the greatest amount of compassion and respect paid to the victims and their families.

This book analyses the minds of those who would commit such horrific crimes.

What drove Ian Brady to kill?
Which serial killer got away with 14 further suspected murders?
Which gangland killer became a successful Scottish artist?

Discover the answers to these questions in this book, where more difficult and devastating truths are also revealed.

THANK YOU

Thank you for reading my book! I always devote a lot of time to making my books as enjoyable as possible for you.

I have a day job working for a lovely charity, so I write on my days off and in the evenings once my daughter has gone to bed and my family duties are done for the day.

So if you enjoyed reading my book, please kindly take a minute to leave a nice review so others can discover me and my writing.

I really appreciate you supporting me as an author and it inspires me to write more books for you!

Amazon: amazon.com/author/aaronmullins

FOLLOW ME

Twitter: twitter.com/DrAaronMullins
Facebook: facebook.com/aaronmullinsauthor
Instagram: instagram.com/draaronmullins
Youtube: youtube.com/c/AaronMullins
Pinterest: pinterest.com/aaronmullinsauthor

READ IT FIRST

Head to my website and click the 'Follow' button to be notified when I publish a new blog post, or a new book!

www.aaronmullins.com